Acclaim f
Andrew G. Marshall

"What he has told me has made me reassess my
relationship behaviour entirely."
—KATY REGAN, *Daily Mail*

"As if someone has just thrown a warm blanket around
my shoulders...it all makes sense."
—HANNAH BOOTH, *Guardian*

"Marshall exudes calm; his voice is gentle and measured"
—TIM DOWLING, *Guardian*

"Andrew G. Marshall offers deeply insightful, helpful, and
practical tools for dealing with most of the challenges we face."
—JED DIAMOND, PH.D., author of *The Irritable Male Syndrome*

"With advice on how to recreate intimacy while retaining a
sense of self...His insightful advice makes it hard to disagree."
—*Psychologies Magazine*
(on *I Love You But I'm Not In Love With You*)

"An insightful and gracious walk through creating positive
change in your life."
—ROBERT J. ACKERMAN, PH.D., Editor, *Counselor Magazine*
(on *Wake Up and Change Your Life*)

PREVIOUS TITLES BY ANDREW G. MARSHALL

ANDREW G. MARSHALL

It's NOT a Midlife  Crisis It's an Opportunity

How to be forty- or fifty-something without going off the rails

MARSHALL METHOD
PUBLISHING

Every reasonable effort has been made to contact copyright holders. If any have been overlooked, the publishers would be glad to hear from them and make good in future editions any errors or omissions brought to their attention.

The case histories in this book are based on couples with whom I have worked in my marital therapy practice (their identities have been changed to protect confidentiality and sometimes two or three cases have been merged together) and individuals who wrote to my website.

If readers have a medical complaint, it is important that they consult their doctor.

Marshall Method Publishing
London • Florida
www.marshallmethodpublishing.com

Library of Congress Cataloging-in-Publication Date is available through the Library of Congress.

ISBN: 978-0-9955403-1-6

Cover and interior design: Gary A. Rosenberg • www.thebookcouple.com

Printed in the United States of America

10 9 8 7 6 5 4 3 2 1

To Ignacio

Contents

Introduction

Is your relationship in crisis or rapidly heading that way? Does it feel like you and your partner have stopped listening to each other and you're either walking on eggshells or exploding with anger? Have you reached the point that you see things so differently you wonder whether it's even worth trying to explain your feelings?

If that doesn't sound bad enough, there's something about being forty- or fifty-something that makes the situation even worse. First of all, the stakes are higher at this stage in your life than at any other. You may have young or adolescent children and you don't want them caught in the crossfire—so you bite your lip and soldier on. Second, your parents are getting old and statistically either you or your partner is likely to have lost one of them. You might even be actively caring for a parent. This is a stark reminder that you are not immortal and, therefore, time is running out. Third, our society is terrified of aging and goes to great lengths to deny it's happening. For example, I appeared on a radio phone-in recently where the host proclaimed that fifty was the new thirty.

So not only is there no road map ahead for the forty- or fifty-somethings among us, but the few signposts that exist are controversial and likely to get you and your partner at each other's throats. I am talking, of course, about the so-called midlife crisis—the logical explanation if your partner has turned into a stranger (and a highly critical one at that), but if you're the one who is questioning your life (and feeling dissatisfied) the term midlife crisis will probably put your back up or make you feel blamed. Whichever side of the debate you stand, I have a radical idea: *it's not a midlife crisis, it's an opportunity* (by which I mean a chance to learn, grow, and transform your life for the better).

I am writing this book from personal and professional experience. I'm fifty-seven and the past twenty years have been, by a long distance, the toughest. However, despite coping with my mother's dementia, my father's frailty, and yesterday catching sight of what at first appeared to be an old man's body in the changing-room mirror of a clothes store, I can honestly say that I have never felt more content, fulfilled, or excited about the future.

Over the course of this book, I will be drawing on my mistakes— embarrassingly many—my setbacks and my heartaches, because I think it is important that you know I've trodden the same path as you rather than having magically arrived at a good place. I will also be drawing on thirty years of experience as a marital therapist helping couples where one partner (and sometimes both) have gone off the rails in their forties or fifties—and done immense damage to themselves and their partner (and often their children too). Fortunately, I have accumulated countless success stories from people who started off in the abyss but returned with a more connected, more satisfying, and more loving relationship. (I have changed names, some of the details and occasionally merged couples to protect identities.)

In each chapter, I will cover a different aspect of being middle-aged—like career issues, depression, affairs, and aging—to explain what is really going on; share relevant scientific research and current psychological and philosophical ideas on the topic; introduce exercises to help you cope better; and teach you new skills to move forward.

The book is divided into three sections. The first is written for people questioning their life, their relationship, and everything. The second is for their partners who are coping with the fallout. Whichever side you're on, *please* read both parts as this will help you understand your partner better and that's an important ingredient for breaking the deadlock. In part three, there is advice about negotiating a way through any differences between you and your partner. I will also introduce three key concepts which will either change your marriage into the connected, fulfilling, and loving relationship of which you've always dreamed or allow you to separate amicably and be great co-parents together.

If you have read my other books the first two concepts will be familiar, but the third I can only teach at this point in your life. Without the necessary life experience, the concept simply goes over people's heads or they go "Yes, but ..." Fortunately, if you have reached forty- or fifty-something, you're ready to be initiated. So please read on ...

Andrew G. Marshall
www.andrewgmarshall.com

PART ONE

How to flourish at forty- or fifty-something and beyond

CHAPTER ONE

The big choice

If the approach of another landmark birthday is sending you into a spiral of depression, you're not alone. I believe it is natural to take stock at the midpoint of your life, but the process can be dispiriting and the view unappetizing. Your career can either feel like you are marking time or that you've reached the promised land—the corner office with people reporting to you, but it's not what you expected. Meanwhile, your friends and contemporaries seem to have levels of success, wealth, and self-confidence that are beyond your reach. You can also feel fed up with your family—taken for granted by your children (or even secretly disappointed by them)—and your relationship, instead of being passionate and connected, is rather stale. Perhaps you've shrugged your shoulders and got on with something more pressing, like your tax return or collecting your daughter from her ballet class.

Except by telling yourself that life begins at forty (or fifty) and ignoring the problems doesn't make them go away. It only takes a crisis—like a restructure at work, redundancy, or the death of a parent—to bring everything back with vengeance. You end up with mood-swings, crippling indecision, and a burning desire to do something else.

Perhaps you sailed through your forties but now younger rivals appear to be snapping at your heels. Or if the age-related paranoia isn't bad enough, maybe you've been busy leading the life that everybody else—your partner, your parents, or society—deems to be right rather than doing what is meaningful to *you*. No wonder you're asking "Does anybody appreciate the sacrifices I've made?" or "Is this is all there is?" or "What's the point?" Maybe there's also someone on the sidelines who makes you feel special, interesting, and young again and you're tempted to do "something just for me" after years of putting other people first.

Alternatively, it could be that your children have left home or are about to fly the nest and the thought of it being just you and your partner is terrifying. What are you going to talk about? There won't just be a conversational hole but an aching gap in your life that used to be filled by the kids. Of course, you could take up some new hobbies or change your job, but time is running out and, quite frankly, you're scared.

I know all about the problems of being middle-aged—and how this can impact on relationships—and not only because 90 percent of the clients at my therapy practice are struggling with it. I lost two jobs that I loved in my late thirties, shortly afterward my partner died and in the aftermath, I did several stupid things. The one that I regret the most was having a short affair with someone in a committed relationship. I thought this would make me feel better (and it did for about two months) but it ended up tipping me into one of the bleakest periods of my life.

So don't worry, I'm not going to judge or preach. I have spent ten years writing about and researching what it is to be forty- or fifty-something and can share the thoughts of some of the greatest minds with you. Also, I know what worked and what didn't work for my clients. I will give you a framework to understand why this phase of your life is so tough, help answer the questions that are plaguing you, and offer suggestions as to how to move forward. Finally, I promise not to tell you what to do. I believe that you are the world's greatest expert on you.

I accept that you're probably still skeptical. Perhaps you've been given this book by some well-meaning friend or your partner has begged you to look at it. I understand your reticence—especially if you're not a big reader—but please read at least this first chapter where I will lay out the main elements and provide a framework to discuss what's been happening in a more positive way.

WHY I HATE THE TERM "MIDLIFE CRISIS"

The term "midlife crisis" was coined as recently as 1965 by the Canadian psychoanalyst and organizational psychologist Elliott Jaques (1917–2003) in an article for the *International Journal of Psychoanalysis* and there has been controversy about whether it exists or not ever since. Part of the problem is that nobody can agree on what constitutes a midlife crisis and the list of symptoms varies. However, they normally include:

- Discontentment or boredom with people and/or activities that provided fulfillment beforehand.

- Feeling restless and wanting to do something completely different with one's life.

- Anxiety about the future.

- Questioning decisions made years earlier and the meaning of life.

- Confusion about who one really is or where one's life is going.

- Daydreaming.

- Irritability, unexpected anger.

- Persistent sadness.

- Increased use of alcohol, drugs, food, or other compulsions.

- Greatly decreased or increased sexual desire.

- Sexual affairs, especially with someone younger.

- Greatly decreased or increased ambition.

- Fretting about status and the point reached in one's career.

- For women in particular, worrying about not having had children or whether they want them in the future.

In fact it's perfectly possible to feel this way or exhibit these behaviors at any age, not just between forty and sixty.

Jaques' original paper was called "Death and the Midlife Crisis." However, I believe that a fear of aging is just one part of the picture (and probably not the most important aspect), as lots of people have a crisis in their middle years without becoming obsessed with death.

Worse still, the midlife crisis has become a joke. I could quote lots of examples but this one sums them up. Question: How do you cover a bald spot? Answer: With a Ferrari. The jokes are usually at the expense of a man, or a woman, having an affair with a tragically younger lover (or lusting after one)—check out the movies *American Beauty* or *The Seven Year Itch* and the media term "cougar" (to describe a hot older woman with a young man). In our society, a midlife crisis is symbolized by buying a fast car, a big motorbike, and other expensive toys or getting a tattoo and ironically adding the hashtag #midlifecrisis on Twitter.

But the greatest problem with the term midlife crisis is that it can be used by one partner to hang all of a couple's relationship problems around the neck of the other. It's almost like they're saying, "It's your fault" or "We'd be fine if it wasn't for you" and "You're acting totally unreasonably"—without asking themselves, "But why is he or she REALLY behaving like this?" or looking at their own contribution. And that's the crux of my issue with midlife crises: the label allows us to stop being curious or compassionate and start blaming. Nobody has ever arrived in my office saying, "Help, I'm having a midlife crisis" but I've had lots of people accusing their partner of having one.

I don't like the word "crisis" because it misses something important: *the opportunity that comes from having a crisis.* The Chinese sign for "crisis" is made up of two characters: danger and opportunity. It is important to get these two elements in balance. Some people only see danger and miss opportunity, while others are so fixed on opportunity that they downgrade or overlook the danger. My aim is to help you steer a wise course between the two.

A DIFFERENT LANGUAGE

To be honest, I didn't want the words midlife crisis on the cover of this book because I find the term misleading. I don't consider what my clients are going through is the punch line of a joke or that they are showing signs of weakness because they can't cope with a few gray hairs. *I believe that stopping and taking stock in middle age is not only necessary but crucial for a happy and satisfying second half of your life.* In fact, when clients arrive in my office struggling with the questions at the heart of this life stage, I am full of admiration (even though their lives have often descended into chaos with affairs, heartbroken children, or clinical depression). I know this response sounds strange but let me explain. These clients are engaging with the truly big issues:

1. Who am I?

2. What are my values?

3. What gives my life meaning?

These are tough question to formulate, let alone answer, and lots of people make a complete mess of it, but that's understandable too. Joseph Campbell (1904–1987) was an American writer and lecturer on comparative mythology and religion who wrote: "A midlife crisis is what happens when you climb to the top of a ladder and discover it's against the wrong wall." Staying with this idea, the majority of the population is keeping busy, distracting themselves while hoping for the best. They might be aware that a ladder exists but they may be too frightened to climb all the way to the top and certainly don't want to look over the wall for fear of what they might find. So if you're currently climbing or poleaxed by the view, you'll find this book extremely reassuring (because although your first reaction might be to destroy the wall, I have some alternatives that will build on the achievements from the first half of your life).

I've wanted to write about the challenges of being middle-aged for a long time but I needed a whole new language. That's why I'm grateful to James Hollis who is a Jungian analyst, a lecturer, and writer. His books include *The Middle Passage: From misery to meaning in midlife* (Inner City Books, 1993). For Hollis, the middle passage is the phase between our first tentative steps into adulthood in our late teens/early twenties and the second half of our life. It begins when the following happens:

- Questioning the partial messages assembled as absolute truths when we were children, teenagers, or when we first tried to make our own way in the world.

- Dealing with issues that have been patched up or ignored from our past.

- Our experience of coming up against the cold, hard realities of life makes us question old certainties or the way everybody else says things should be done.

- Identity issues are coming to the fore.

I like the term middle passage—and that's what I'm going to use throughout the book—because it uncouples the idea of questioning your life according to your age. You can go through the middle passage in your twenties (the quarter-life crisis), in your forties and fifties (the midlife crisis), or even later. The other advantage of the middle passage is that it's perfectly possible to pass through it without a crisis. However, I would argue that's difficult because our society discourages us from asking awkward questions. When everything gets pushed underground, the underlying problems become entrenched and the chances of an emotional meltdown dramatically increase.

THE U-SHAPED LIFE

I think the best way to understand the middle passage is by putting it into the context of our whole lives. I've spent thirty years listening to people talk about their childhoods and the vast majority report it was good or happy. Even if their circumstances were diffi-cult—perhaps their parents argued incessantly or they had a destruc-tive relationship with one or both parents—they told themselves, with all the confidence of youth, that they "wouldn't make the same mistakes" or they would "make better choices."

When I discussed her childhood with Natalie, thirty-five, she talked about the pain of her parents' divorce and how she dealt with the fallout by immersing herself in books: "I was a terrible dreamer and I loved fairytales where everybody lived happily ever after. My reading habit exploded when I was about nine after we abruptly came back from a family vacation—because my father was flirting so openly with another woman on the caravan site. My parents split up and never really spoke to each other again. My brother and I were shuttled back and forth at motorway rest areas or my father would hoot the car outside the house. Within a couple of years, I would escape into adult novels—like *Jane Eyre*—where love would always come through and right everything. The real world might have seemed drab and unhappy but I could cope by escaping into these multicolored parallel universes.'

When you're young, the solutions to a crisis seem within your grasp. Mike was thirty-nine when he started coming to me and reported having had the standard "good" childhood. I doubt your father dying when you were ten, the family business going bust, and having to move in with your paternal grandparents (who didn't really get on with your mother) would be most people's definition of "good." So how did Mike keep afloat when he was effectively small and powerless in a big and frightening world?

"I told my mom, I'm going to grow up and make lots of money and buy you a house—just like the one that we lost," he explained to me. So he worked hard at school, passed his exams, and became a banker (just like the man who recalled his parents' loans after his father died and repossessed his childhood home).

Whatever the circumstances, most people felt loved by at least one of their parents or someone significant when they were young and therefore have some positive memories on which to draw. There are ways of looking at the world during childhood that offer protection against the harsh realities of life and keep most of us psychologically healthy. (I will explain how they might have seemed appropriate when we were young, but need updating during middle age.)

Therefore, most people start their journey through life in a positive place. Think of it as the beginning of the U. Adolescence can be difficult and testing but we still have plenty of time to become the CEO of a leading international company, a famous movie star, score the winning goal at a baseball game, find a cure for cancer, or write the novel that is going to define our generation. We are also going to fall in love, finding someone who completely understands us, and recognizes our true value. Our children are going to be not only beautiful, well-behaved, and successful but will appreciate all the sacrifices we'll make for them. There might be tremors in our twenties where we have our heart broken or don't get the job that we were set on or our baby cries through the night, every night, but it's easy to overlook these disruptions. Life is full and the road ahead beckons.

In the same way that the first part of life is generally good, the last section can be equally satisfying. Research into older people, aged sixty plus, points to them being the section of the population most likely to feel fulfilled. For example, the University of Chicago tracked 28,000 people between 1972 and 2004 and found that once they had made allowances for the ups and downs of economic fortune, which affected everyone, older people were the happiest. Indeed, the odds of being happy increased with every ten years of age. Similar results were found by Florida State University College of Medicine who studied 2,300 people with an average age of sixty-nine, living in Baltimore, between 1979 and 2010. The research was led by Angelina Sutin who summed up their findings:

"Especially when we're young, it's really easy to look at older adults and see the loss: loss of youth, loss of mobility, loss of loved ones. We assume that all of that loss would make older adults unhappy. It's harder to see the benefits of aging: feelings of pride for children and grandchildren, a meaningful career, more confidence, wisdom. There are a lot of reasons to be happy in older adulthood."

In the UK, the Office for National Statistics collected data from 300,000 adults between 2012 and 2015 and found life satisfaction improving from 60 plus, and the age group with the most positive ratings aged 70–74.

In my experience, older people's relationships tend to be stronger and this stage can be a mirror of when they started out. When we first fall in love, we're buoyed up the fantasy of our future lives as a couple. Later, our love is supported by the memories of a life spent together and the strength that comes from overcoming obstacles along the way. If you want to see a truly romantic couple—look at a pair who are sixty or seventy plus. No wonder the makers of *When Harry met Sally* peppered their movie with interviews with just these couples. Older people have time to follow their interests, study what intrigues them (rather than worrying about passing exams), to travel the world, and even if money is tight, at least they don't have to battle their way through the morning rush hour to work every day. They have more choices and that can lead to greater satisfaction. Think of this time as the second upward swing of the U.

The toughest part of life is usually the middle section: the trough at the center of the U-shaped life. In the Office for National Statistics research quoted earlier, life satisfaction plummets around 35, and 40- to 49-year-olds are the most anxious age group. It's hard earning a living, bringing up children, running a house, and still finding enough time for what makes you happy. Even worse, the optimism of your early twenties has been tempered by new realities.

For example, my first career was in commercial radio. When I left university, in the early eighties, it was a time of great expansion. New stations were coming on air in big cities and towns, and that offered lots of opportunity for promotion and good salaries. However, by my mid-thirties, a recession, consolidation (where radio stations shared programs), and new technology (which lead to fewer staff) meant an entirely different outlook. The recession from 2007 onward had a devastating effect on the industry and shed thousands of jobs. Most of the radio stations that I worked for subsequently disappeared and when I recently went to an old staff reunion only a handful of my former colleagues still worked in radio.

Relationships can be put under a lot of pressure in our forties and fifties. Your children may have become teenagers—a time when parents are no longer at the center of their lives and are sometimes even downright embarrassing! You are also facing the reality of your own parents getting frailer and maybe even confused. They need more of your precious time and it's easy to feel squeezed by the pressures of the generation below and the generation above—the classic sandwich generation. And if you're not careful, you or your partner can feel that you've slipped down each other's list of priorities as well.

All those years ago, you fell in love because you had fun together and you got married to officially spend more time together. Nowadays, it seems all you do is tick off items on a neverending to do list or maybe snipe at each other. In the little time left over for fun, you're too exhausted for much beyond watching TV together or sharing a bottle of wine. In the words of the poet Thomas Moore (1779–1852), your relationship is not "love's young dream."

A CASE HISTORY

A good example of someone struggling with the complexities of the middle passage is James, a 55-year-old engineer with two grown-up children in their twenties and a younger daughter of 15. He had separated from his wife of thirty years and felt uncertain about whether they had a future together.

"Our sex life was poor for a long time and over the past five years had dwindled down to nothing," he told me. "I've tried to be positive and keep the peace at home but that's meant doing what everybody else wants until I felt I could only be true to myself for about five percent of the time. If we had an argument, my wife would get angry, explode, and threaten to leave so I'd back down." Although this approach had kept their marriage functioning and the children happy, it came at a terrible cost: "I had this ball of resentment across half of my chest. It used to be a molten rock but now it's a cold one full of guilt for not feeling emotionally attached to my wife."

Meanwhile his wife, 53-year-old Patty, was upset but determined to save their marriage:

"I've been very naive," she said. "I thought James was unhappy with work and I put the reason that he wouldn't talk down to him being private. So I absorbed myself in bringing up the children."

In fact, James was showing all the key indicators for someone encountering the middle passage:

- *Challenging partial messages from childhood assembled as absolute truths:* "I started work at thirteen mowing neighbors' lawns and I thought if I worked hard and provided then everybody would be happy and that would make me happy," said James. "Today, I find my job restricting, uninteresting, and unrewarding but I'm trapped because it pays the bills and provides the lifestyle everybody has got used to."

  Although we are told that hard work will be rewarded, this is a partial rather than an absolute truth.

- *Issues that have been patched up coming to the fore:* "I would dearly like to fall back in love with my wife because that would make everybody happy and, at heart, I'm a people-pleaser, but I can't just change my feelings," James explained. The fundamental issue in the marriage of James and Patty was communication. In particular, he would bottle his feelings (which made her feel that everything was OK) and she would blow up (which made him prioritize her feelings over his in the hope of avoiding a row). The result was lots of important issues had been buried—in some cases for ten years or more. For example, James would much rather have joined his parents for big family Christmases with his siblings and their children but they lived a long distance away and it had seldom happened. Patty remembered things differently:

'But we did go on a couple of occasions,' she protested, 'and I thought you were happy creating our own family traditions."

"But my parents missed out on knowing all of their grand-children and our kids never got to know them either," replied James.

In effect, he had buried his unhappiness about their Christmas arrangements, but the middle passage brought them back to the surface.

■ *Life experiences making us challenge messages from parents, society etc:* "Leaving my wife and children goes against everything I was taught by my parents, the church, and society. It's not what a good man does, he stands up and is counted." James had been living by everybody else's code and hadn't really thought about his own values and beliefs because, as a people-pleaser, he had trained himself to be acutely aware of other people's opinions and to downgrade his own. The result was that he had a big house packed with consumer goodies and had to work extremely hard to financially service everything. "I've started to question if I really need to be dragging all this stuff behind me. What would my life be like without all this debt?"

Unfortunately, instead of following this line of thinking—which would probably have been productive and avoided his meltdown—he just threw all of his parents' and society's values out of the window and had an affair. Our task during counseling was to find the right balance between being completely selfish (and considering nobody else beyond himself) and being so altruistic (and worried about other people's needs) that he felt empty inside.

■ *Identity issues taking centerstage:* "My father died recently, which has been really hard because I loved him dearly," explained James, "and that's got me thinking: I'm now the head of the family—the patriarch. I'm no longer somebody's son. What does that mean? What am I going to do with the rest of my life?"

This is what makes a midlife relationship crisis so difficult to unpick—and therefore so dangerous. Like the question, what came first, the chicken or the egg? How much of James' crisis was down to relationship problems and how much personal problems?

While James was stuck in the middle of the trough in the U-shaped life, his wife was suffering too: "I'm struggling with similar issues myself. My youngest child will soon be off my hands and that's a great hole in our life, but also a great opportunity," Patty stated. "What am I going to do next? What's going to give my life meaning?"

So we started on improving their communication (encouraging James to be more forthcoming and Patty to listen properly rather than getting upset about what she thought he'd said). We also looked at the problems from the past (so the ghosts could have a proper burial) and discussed how they might work as a team to solve their individual identity issues (rather than undermining each other). I will be returning to James and Patty so you can get a better idea of what this involves.

EXERCISE   NAME YOUR THOUGHT PATTERNS

The middle passage requires us to take stock of our lives, face up to any disappointments, and answer difficult questions. This requires a lot of thinking. Unfortunately, our culture is not particularly comfortable with thinking—much preferring men of action or women who "know their own mind." Meanwhile, intellectuals are dismissed as out of touch with real life, and personal introspection is considered suspect or ridiculed as "sitting cross-legged halfway up a mountain lighting joss sticks" or "contemplating your own navel."

Despite all these negative messages, we have thousands of thoughts every day and yet how we solve problems and the full implications of what we're thinking is seldom examined. It's almost as if we're on autopilot and, beyond a vague sense of disappointment or unease, not fully conscious. So the first exercise, in this book, gives you permission to think and encourages you to become more mindful of your thought patterns.

When you're lost in thought or your mind is turning over something that happened in the past or might happen in the future, I'd like you to be curious about the nature of these thoughts. How does your mind work? Does it latch onto one particular subject or is it like a snowball rolling down a mountain gathering more and more topics? (Or perhaps a frog jumping from issue to issue). When do you think: in the middle of the night, in the gaps between being busy (like when you are driving the car, walking up the stairs), all the time, or only when you're tired? Don't judge your thoughts, there is no right or wrong approach, but I would like you to name your thought patterns. Here are some of the ways that my clients have described their thinking:

- Anxious thoughts (worried about how to cope with something or coming up with lots of obstacles: "I'll never find anywhere to park").

- Catastrophic or hopeless thoughts (coming up with the worst possible scenario: "It's sure to be cancer" or "It's all downhill from here").

- Self-critical thoughts (pointing out what you've done wrong: "I should have set off earlier").

- Self-punishing thoughts (this often leads on from self-critical thinking but at the center is a sense of personal worthlessness: "I'm stupid, inconsiderate [etc]." If anybody else said these things, you would stand up for yourself but because it's coming from inside your head, it is somehow honest and true).

- Self-limiting thoughts (you dismiss ideas before they're fully formed: "I wouldn't know where to start" or "I can't start a business because I'm hopeless at finances").

- Daydreaming (looking forward to a time in the future: "It'll be wonderful when ..." or "I can't wait to get home and ...").

- Planning thinking ("What are we going to eat tonight?" or "I'll phone Mom when I've put the kids to bed").

- Morbid thoughts (these dwell on aging, decay, and death: "I'm getting moles across my chest" or "I have these flapping wings under my arms now").

- Negative thoughts (random elements from different parts of your life are often tied together to make a cast-iron case: "I didn't get that promotion" and "My partner didn't want sex this morning" and "I forgot to collect that package from the post office" becomes "My life is a complete mess").

- Cheerleading (this could be general exhortations to yourself like "no pain, no gain" or wisdom taken from the Internet, but you're always trying to boost yourself up).

- Creative thinking (when you're brainstorming solutions to a problem, trying to solve a puzzle, or indulging in some artistic or craft-based activity).

- Inspired thinking (while creative thinking is done consciously, this thought pattern often starts up when your mind is half engaged on something else—like going for a run—and suddenly a solution or an idea just pops into your head).

- Thinking-thinking (when you're going through the options, considering where to get further advice, or weighing up an argument).

There is no right or wrong approach. You might also come up with different terms that better sum up how you think. The aim of this exercise is to become aware of your thought patterns and how your brain works. So next time your mind gets going, start to identify the thought patterns: "Oh, that's anxious thinking" or "Here we go again, self-limiting thinking." For the time being, just witness your thoughts and (I know this is hard) try not to judge yourself.

THE W-SHAPED LIFE

Many men and women, when they reach middle age, will recognize the sentiment behind this famous quote from the American writer and philosopher Henry David Thoreau (1817–1862): "The mass of men lead lives of quiet desperation." Unfortunately, our culture does not encourage too much self-analysis and sometimes even considers it subversive. We tend to keep our heads down and carry on regardless.

There's always plenty of pressing matters clamoring for our attention: our inbox is full, the children have exams, and the car needs servicing. Except ignoring problems makes them worse and, once again, Thoreau hits the nail on the head: "What is called resignation is confirmed desperation."

To compound the problem, our brains are constructed in a way that it makes it harder to answer the existential questions of the middle passage. Daniel Kahneman is an Israeli-American psychologist who has studied how we make decisions. He was awarded the 2002 Nobel Prize in Economic Sciences and is considered the father of behavioral economics. In his bestselling book *Thinking, Fast and Slow* (Penguin, 2012), he explains how our brains use two modes. He calls them system one (which happens quickly and automatically and with no effort or sense of voluntary control) and system two (which allocates our attention to complex mental activities). Although we think of ourselves as rational (centered in system two), we tend to use reactive thinking (centered in system one) most of the time—especially when strong emotions like fear, love, or hatred are evoked. For important decisions, we might imagine that we use system two (the reasoning and cautious approach) but Kahneman has found that we operate on the law of least effort, and that we generally gravitate toward the path that offers the least resistance.

So how does this apply to the middle passage? When faced with tough questions like "Who am I?" or "What gives my life meaning?" —which I need a whole book to tackle—it's not surprising that we opt for something easy. For example, "Do I enjoy flirting with this coworker?" and "Would it be fun to go for a drink together?" and "Do I fancy him?" or "Do I want to sleep with her?" Although our rational system two brain knows that we are heading into dangerous territory, in the words of Kahneman it is a "lazy controller" and does not bother to calculate the risks to our financial wellbeing, the upset of our partner, or the long-term impact on our children. Instead, system one is in charge and (maybe fueled by alcohol and lust) is opting for the simplest question of all: "Will this make me feel good?" especially as "Most of the time I am desperately unhappy."

Returning to James and Patty, his job took him all over the world, and on one particular business trip to Eastern Europe, he met a much younger woman. They quickly established a good connection. "I could be myself with her," explained James. "She didn't judge me and I felt she knew me better than Patty." They went on to have an affair for three years and eventually James sponsored her to come to London as a student. Although James felt that his life was finally on the upswing again, trying to please two women at the same time became increasingly difficult.

"My girlfriend wanted me to tell my wife but I didn't want to break Patty's heart. My father fell ill and I had taken a leave of absence from work to fly off to be by his bedside. I would come out of a five-hour stretch in the acute ward with my father and find a string of texts from my girlfriend saying 'Where are you?' and 'You promised to always be there for me.'" At this point his girlfriend started to withdraw, returned to her home country, and became involved with another man. His wife uncovered the affair and he moved out of the marital home into a small apartment.

Instead of James coming out of the trough of the U-shaped life, as he had hoped by having an affair, he had fallen right back: "I'm still in contact with my girlfriend and we regularly text each other—even though she is about to get married. We had lunch the other day when she visited London. I know I risk undermining her forth-coming marriage—we tell each other we'll stop after her wedding day—and it makes Patty despair about anything changing, but I can't let go. It's a complete and utter mess."

Not only did James experience only a temporary lift to his mood, he still faced all the familiar problems of the middle passage—finding meaning in his life, dealing with the loss of his father, and getting to know himself properly. His affair had not been the answer but a short-lived distraction. It's a phenomenon that I see over and over again and refer to as the W-shaped life: a short upswing followed by a fall back into the trough of despair. When economists draw a graph for falling stock prices, they sometimes call this blip a "dead cat bounce." What they mean by this colorful image is that if you drop a dead cat from a great height it will still bounce and gives the momentary illusion of being alive (as prices may appear to recover). When James started counseling, he had reached the second dip of the W and still needed to climb out and repair his life.

It's not just affairs that provide a short-lived boost. It could be quitting your job on a whim and throwing yourself into a reckless business opportunity or deciding to move to the other side of the world (but finding that you've brought all the old problems with you). Obviously it is regrettable to put so much time, energy, and money into something that later proves to be the wrong solution—and let's not forget the heartache to yourself and your nearest and dearest—but at least with the W-shaped life, you do *finally* engage with the tough questions of the middle passage and therefore still reap the benefits of a happy and fulfilled second half of your life.

THE L-SHAPED LIFE

Although the U-shaped life is hard and the W-shaped life comes with a lot of collateral damage, there is a worse option. I call this the L-shaped life because some people never engage with the issues of the middle passage. Instead they anesthetize themselves against the disappointment and quiet desperation of being middle-aged with drink, recreational drugs, or other self-medicating activities like gambling, compulsive shopping, or immersive computer games. Alternatively, they become cynical, bitter, and closed off. These people's motto is "won't be fooled again" and they gain a small amount of satisfaction from pouring cold water on other people's plans. They comfort themselves with the idea that everything is fixed (so there's no point in applying for that new job) and nobody appreciates them (so there's no point in changing) and they read newspapers and blogs confirming the notion that we're all going to hell in a handcart. When something goes wrong, they blame other people and assume that the world is against them. Instead of enjoying the benefits of being older, because they are not open to change or new ideas, they end up grumpy old men or women. In effect, they don't engage with the tough questions of life and remain forever trapped on the wrong side of the middle passage: disillusioned, maybe struggling with untreated depression or turning into an aging Peter or Princess Pan (the female equivalent).

Sadly, I think the L-shaped life is what a lot of people settle for— hence my admiration for clients struggling through the middle passage. The full extent of opting out is perhaps best illustrated by our gradual disengagement from politics. In the UK, at the 1950 general election the turnout was 83.9%, by 1979 (and the election of Mrs Thatcher) it was 76% but by 2001 it was down to just 59.4% (although the figures have rallied slightly since). Opinion polls report that we're disillusioned and feel the main parties are not listening to us (perhaps because less than 1% of us belong to them and almost one in four of us don't vote) or that we feel it's a pointless exercise because they are all the same. Some people join single-issue pressure groups or are involved in some form of direct action, but the vast majority don't believe that change is possible (unless it's for the worse). Alternatively, they opt for unlikely outsider parties and candidates— on either the extreme left or right—who concentrate on blaming the 'establishment' rather than laying out credible alternatives.

EXERCISE **RECLAIM YOUR LIFE**

Think back to the last period in your life when you felt generally happy or when your life seemed less frantic. Spend some time remembering. You might like to switch your phone off and close your eyes.

- Picture this past time in detail. How old are you? Where are you?

- Reconstruct your life: were there particular activities that you did on certain days? How did you spend your time?

- Pinpoint what brought you pleasure, provided excitement, or maybe even purpose.

- What did you particularly enjoy?

Once you've got a good picture of what nourished you in the past, open your eyes and get out a piece of paper (or take notes on your phone).

- In the first column I'd like you to record these pleasurable activities.

- Now put a tick beside everything that you still do.

- How many have disappeared out of your life or are only done on rare occasions?

- Next, turn to the second column and list everything that currently depletes you (these are activities that drain you in some way).

- Add tasks that you feel that you should or must do (for example, checking emails before going to bed)—these are probably depleting you too.

Finally, take one item from your nourishing list and commit to doing it in the coming week.

This exercise will help you to get back in touch with something that you've lost along the way between childhood and middle age. I'd also like you to take one item from your draining list and either cut down the number of times that you perform this task or simply drop it altogether for a week. In this way, you can start to find a better balance in your life.

MAKING THE BIG CHOICE

I've called this chapter the big choice because that's what we face in our forties and fifties. Do we engage with the important questions of life or simply distract ourselves with short-term pleasures? Do we learn to communicate effectively with our partner and try to live in a more fulfilling way or do we opt for the easy life (choosing not to bring up difficult and potentially upsetting topics)? Are we prepared to take a fresh look at ourselves and find new challenges or just keep busy and look the other way? Can we identify what's within our power to change or do we simply rail against the system? Do we go for a quick fix—like plastic surgery or the vacation of a lifetime—or opt for the hard work of forging a more meaningful life?

I know these are really tough choices and the impact of climbing the ladder and looking over the wall can be terrifying. (Don't worry, I'm going to break everything down into manageable chunks, teaching you new skills and fresh approaches.) Hopefully, you're beginning to understand why being middle-aged is such an important phase and feel excited by the prospect of the upward curve of the U-shaped life. Please read on.

SUMMING UP

➤ If you're struggling with the issues of being middle-aged, it's not a sign of weakness or self-indulgence but something positive.

➤ The middle passage is the difficult but necessary transition at the center of the U-shaped life.

➤ Instead of discovering what would make life meaningful, many people go for what would make them happy today, but risk sliding back down again (the W-shaped life); or they simply close down and become cynical and don't benefit from the uplift in the second half of their life at all (the L-shaped life).

CHAPTER TWO

How did I get here?

In the last chapter, I explained the concept of the middle passage and why being middle-aged is one of the toughest life stages, but I wouldn't be surprised if you're still wondering why everything seems so heavy-going (maybe you flew through previous difficult transitions like school, university, and forging a career). Therefore, I'm going to break down the challenges of each of your previous life stages and explain the ways of thinking that helped you then but now risk tipping your life into chaos. I'm also going to look at the outside forces that have shaped you: your family, our wider culture, and events that might have blown you off course and left a lasting legacy. First, I want to offer a little reassurance.

It's easy to think that everybody else has their life sorted. I've fallen into that trap myself. As a therapist, I did realize that everybody else doesn't know what they're doing (because otherwise I'd be out of a job) but I used to imagine that there were lots of other people living the good life. Particularly in my late thirties and early forties, I felt really frustrated. I couldn't seem to get the breaks in my career. There was a small voice in my head that whispered, "You're not good enough" or "You're not part of the in crowd." Whatever the cause, I just couldn't make it to the promised land.

If I'd been asked to name one of the people who had it cracked, I'd probably have said Leonard Cohen (the singer, songwriter, and poet). After all, he had been loved by some of the most beautiful women of his era, sold millions of albums, written songs that have been covered by countless other artists (and brought him riches beyond my imagination) and he had a loyal following of fans around the world. He is also an intelligent and spiritual man who was ordained as a Rinzai Zen Buddhist monk in 1996. So I was fascinated to read an interview to celebrate his eightieth birthday where he stated: "Everybody has experienced defeat in their lives. Nobody had a life that worked out the way they wanted it to."

THE LEGACY OF YOUR CHILDHOOD

When you were a small child you probably thought you were the center of the universe, and that's healthy. After all, as a baby, you must start by discovering yourself, putting your fingers in your mouth, playing with your toes, and then when you're a bit older crawling off to discover the world around you. Right from the beginning, you're getting messages about your general acceptability from your parents and caregivers. You smiled and your mother smiled back and that was reassuring. You stuck out your hand and your father put out his hand. It felt good to connect. However, our young brains are not sufficiently developed to step into another person's shoes or to understand the pressures someone else might be under. So if you fell over and cried and your mother or father didn't come running right away or they were upset with you for falling, in your half-formed brain you could have concluded you'd done something wrong (or there was something wrong with you). You didn't have enough experience to know they were probably angry with themselves for being momentarily distracted or frightened about what could have happened.

Magical thinking

When we are young, we have very little control over our lives. We have to eat what our parents give us, go where they take us, and do what they say. We have some limited agency when we throw a tantrum or sulk (refusing to do what they want) or pester and wheedle (attempting to manipulate them), but our power to influence is on the margins. Furthermore, the world around is complicated and there's lots that we can't understand. It would be easy to become completely overwhelmed and frightened. Fortunately, most of us are lucky enough to have our parents around to make the right decisions for us (until we're old enough to make them for ourselves).

There's another factor that comes to our rescue: magical thinking. When I was about five, I remember thinking that I was beginning to understand how things worked and in a short time I would know everything. The thought was so strong that I can even remember where I was (outside our house walking up the passage to the side gate). I would soon know how my parents "made" my sister and understand why they had smiled when I asked how they could be sure they wouldn't make another sister. How was I going to understand "everything?" Somehow the knowledge was going to settle on my shoulders like an invisible cloak—almost like magic. I was a shy child but magical thinking gave me the confidence to ask questions and to believe that I could make sense of the answers.

Children often have to deal with more distressing experiences than the birth of a sibling. Many of my clients are on the verge of splitting up and turning their sons' and daughters' lives upside down. Jonas, thirty-five, has been asked to leave by his wife because she "needed space" and for him to stop "pressurizing" her about whether she still loved him or not.

"My son is four and has been really worried about where I will go," he reported, "so he made a nest of his toys and blankets in his room and said I could sleep there." Instead of feeling overwhelmed, Jonas' son had used magical thinking to provide a solution. His father could live in the corner of his bedroom instead.

In the case of Claire, forty, her daughter (also five) had found an equally magical solution to the news that her father had moved around the corner. Claire explained: "She's been draping fabrics in her bedroom and moving the lamps around. The other day she told me, 'I'm making my bedroom really pretty so Daddy won't go.' It broke my heart."

On one hand it's so sad that these children are suffering, but it's also wonderful that they are engaging with the problem and trying to find a solution (to the best of their ability). Obviously, there is a problem with magical thinking. If Jonas moves out, his son might conclude that his nest was not comfortable enough; Claire's daughter may assume that her bedroom was not fabulous enough to keep her dad's attention.

Downside at middle age

What works at five is not so effective at fifty-five. When I'm faced with a crisis now, I know I'm not the center of the world and I don't have magical powers. After my partner died, when I was thirty-seven, I used to torture myself by wishing I'd insisted on going to the doctor sooner or another scenario where one random change in my choices would have created a parallel world with a happy ending. (Fortunately, I talked over these thoughts with friends who helped me realize how misguided they were.)

My clients are often struggling with a similar legacy. Jeanette, forty, had been adopted as a child. Having finally decided to trace her biological parents, she discovered that her father had died a few years after her birth. She arrived in my counseling office the following week convinced her birth had catapulted him out of college, turned him into a lost boy, and sent him off to a remote region of India where he had contracted a stomach bug and died.

"I can't help thinking that if I hadn't been born, he'd still be alive and well," she told me.

We looked at the choices of her biological parents (they didn't use contraception), the decisions of her biological mother's parents (they put pressure on her to give up the child for adoption), but still Jeanette felt in some way responsible. I reminded Jeanette that she wasn't the center of the universe, and eventually she admitted that her father was an adult who had made his own choices. She was in tears but beginning to let go of the self-blame.

The idea that we *should* be able to control everything is very strong. There's a legendary moment from the original *Star Trek* series when Captain Kirk is asking the engine room for more power and Scotty the engineer tells him: "I can't change the laws of physics." Deep down, we know Scotty is right but we can't help but wish it was otherwise.

I hear a lot of magical thinking in middle age. For example: "If I really believe in this new enterprise it is bound to be successful" (even though you haven't researched its viability or written a business plan) or "The kids will get on fine with my new girlfriend" (even though you're planning on leaving their mother for her) or "If only we could get away and spend some time together we would be able to reconnect" (even though there are fundamental problems in your marriage).

Of course, a new job, a new relationship, or a good vacation might be part of a more meaningful future, but on their own they are not going to magically transform your life. You still need to roll up your sleeves and do the heavy lifting.

THE LEGACY OF OUR ADOLESCENCE

Going to school and meeting other children and teachers, who aren't always impressed with us, can be a shock. We get the first inkling that we might not be the center of the universe and some of our rougher edges get knocked off. But for some children, especially those who don't feel they fit in at home, school can be a pleasant surprise. There is an alternative world out there and it is beckoning to us.

As we head toward adolescence we're depending less on our parents for both our physical and psychological wellbeing. The opinions of our peers and popular culture (which is greatly influenced by other adolescents) becomes increasingly important. We're not ready to leave the nest but are beginning to wonder about our place in the wider world. Parents' friends or relatives ask us what we want to do when we grow up, we explore careers guidance at school, and we may have long chats into the night with our friends about the meaning of life.

It can be a heady and exciting time but it's also frightening. It's the first time that we've really begun to struggle with identity issues and asked "Who am I?" The problems are confounded by having only limited knowledge about how the world works (outside the confined world of school, college, and university). How do you make your own way in the world? How do you become an adult?

Joseph Campbell, whom we met in the last chapter, studied anthropologists' accounts of tribes whose way of life had not been corrupted by exposure to Western culture. He was interested in the rituals for the important moments in life—like marriage, birth of a child, death—and something lost in the modern world: initiation into the tribe through a rite of passage. This would involve separation from parents, a ritual kidnapping where a boy would be taken from the village by the older men, and a girl by the older women. There would be some sort of ordeal or test and the adolescent would be taught the myths of the tribe and what it meant to become a man or a woman. After this ritual death of childhood and rebirth away from the community, the adolescents would return to their parents as adults.

For Jewish teenagers there is the bar mitzvah and bat mitzvah, and in the US and Canada and some Latin countries a sweet sixteen party is held for girls, but generally contemporary culture does not mark the transition from adolescent to young adult (perhaps because it takes so much longer) and what remains is often stripped of real meaning.

In his influential book *The Hero with a Thousand Faces* (originally published in 1949), Campbell explains that we have two viable options at adolescence. The first is to be a hero and forge our own path in the world and become "a personage of not only local but historical moment." The second is a less adventurous civic route—bringing up a family, offering service to the community, being a good man or woman—but this is made meaningful by the inherited myths, symbols, and rites of passage handed down through the millennia. Unfortunately, in Campbell's opinion, most of us don't easily fall into either category: "It is only those who know neither an inner call nor an outer doctrine whose plight is truly desperate; that is to say, most of us today, in this labyrinth without and within the heart. Alas, where is the guide?"

Heroic thinking

The world is large and we're small and frightened; fortunately we have another valuable tool at our disposal: heroic thinking. This is best encapsulated by the hit theme song from *Fame*. In it, kids from the New York High School of Performing Arts sing that they are going to live forever and are going to learn how to fly. Just to be sure that we've got the message, they tell us to remember their name. I was twenty-one when the movie came out and I bought the sound-track and sung along without once remarking that nobody lives forever and human beings can't fly. So I'm going to share one piece of my heroic thinking from this era. My ambition at university was to have a career in radio, and I remember clearly thinking that I could become director-general of the BBC.

It's wonderful that we tell young people they can be anything they want, but without heroic thinking they would not believe us. It is this power that gets us off our parents' couch and out into the world. (Of course, I didn't become director-general but I did have a long career in radio and held several senior posts.)

Another popular form of heroic thinking is "I'm not going to make the same mistakes as my parents." This comes in many forms: "I'm going to find someone who truly loves me" or "I'm not going to settle for dull suburbia" or just a general "They'll all be sorry some day." We're not certain quite how it will happen, but our general fabulousness will be recognized and we'll be raised up to our true place in society.

Downside at middle age

While it is great to want to be director-general in your teens, to still be hankering after it in middle age would be tragic—and would probably leave you in some dark corner muttering about the unfair-ness of life. Interestingly, I interviewed Sir Michael Checkland (who was director-general of the BBC 1987–1992) and I didn't feel even one moment of jealousy. In retrospect I would have hated a job tied down by bureaucracy and politics with limited opportunities for creativity.

I see a lot of heroic thinking in my middle-aged clients. Simon, forty-three, loved his wife and their two children but unfortunately he also had a girlfriend who had recently had his baby. Worse still, his wife had no idea that he was being unfaithful or that he had a secret family who also needed his support.

"I kept telling myself there has to be some solution," he explained after everything had come out and he and his wife started counseling. "I thought I would become a property developer—the next Donald Trump—and make millions and keep everybody happy."

"How was that going to work?" his wife Rachel asked. "You think we'd all go, 'Fine, Simon, do whatever you want' just because you threw some money about?"

"I don't know, it all seems madness now," he said, and looked down at the floor.

And that's the problem with heroic thinking: it allows you to find both a magical solution *and* a plausible cover story to avoid dif-ficult questions and let you get on with day-to-day business—in Simon's case trying to be in two places at the same time, holding down a demanding job, and preventing his secret from coming out. Would money have stopped his wife from being angry about his infidelity? Would it have prevented his girlfriend from being upset that he wouldn't leave his wife? How would he have borrowed enough capital to get going without his wife finding out? How long would it have taken to make a Donald Trump-style fortune and did he have that much time? I could go on. Under the spell of heroic thinking, you can do anything you want, so you don't need to know exactly how your goal will be achieved or whether your goal is even the right one.

THE LEGACY OF PROVISIONAL ADULTHOOD

If nobody takes us off into the woods and sits us around a camp-fire and explains how things work, and if we have no clear sense of who we are—because we're growing, changing, and trying on different identities, how do we become an adult? The answer is that we copy what other adults do: find a job, get married, and start our own family. It's almost like saying, "I pay my taxes now, therefore I must be an adult." However, part of being an adult is knowing your own mind and what's right for you, rather than blithely following the pack. That's why I call this phase provisional adulthood, because we've got our learner plates on, and we're trying out different jobs and relationships in order to find our place in the world.

Returning to my own experience, I started work as a radio reporter in the 24-hour newsroom of a large city radio station; but I soon found arriving at an event, making a 45-second report and dashing on to the next story unsatisfying. I wanted to go behind the surface. Thirty plus years later, in the middle of writing an 80,000-word book, this discovery seems blindingly obvious, but my provisional adult had to find that out for himself.

Not only do we copy what other adults do in our provisional adulthood, we also invest in their roles. Our job soon defines us. We are someone's husband or wife. We are someone's father or mother. We rarely question whether we're more than the sum of our accumulated roles. We are going to make our mark on the world, love is going to save us, our children will give us a sense of purpose, and everything will be fine. So what could possibly go wrong?

"Events my dear boy, events," said Harold Macmillan (British Prime Minister 1957–1963), when questioned by a journalist about what was most likely to blow a government off course. This applies to our lives too. Our employer goes bankrupt or relocates to the other side of the globe; someone else get the promotion that we set our heart on; the birth of a second child brings back uncomfortable memories from our own childhood; our parent dies and we realize that we never really knew him or her; we have a nasty car crash, can't exercise for eighteen months, and feel like a caged animal; our partner has been having a secret Facebook conversation with his or her first love. The list of possible events is endless.

Wishful thinking

I know I am going to state the obvious but, in the words of the American poet Henry Wadsworth Longfellow (1807–1882): "Into each life some rain must fall." Although we know the truth of this, we want to believe that we are somehow immune. We look at the statistics, for example, on infidelity—55% of people in the UK admitted adultery at some point in their lives (British Sexual Fantasy Research Project 2007), while the Kinsey research into American sexuality in the forties and fifties found 26% of married women and 50% of married men had cheated on their spouse—but we still think it won't happen to us. Meanwhile, one in four adults experience a mental health issue every year, according to the Health and Social Care Centre Survey. In 2009, this included 2.6% of the population suffering from depression, 4.7% with anxiety, and 9.7% with mixed anxiety and depression. The figures are frightening but we look the other way.

We hear the quote by the British Politician Enoch Powell (1912–1998): "all political lives end in failure, because that is the nature of politics and of human affairs" and think it does apply to our field of work or we'll be the exception to the rule. So how do we avoid looking at dark and dreary truth?

To protect ourselves, we practi"e wishful thinking. In other words, 'I won't lose my job because my talent will protect me" or "My partner wouldn't be unfaithful because I'm a good spouse" or "Good things happen to good people (and I'm a good person)" or "My love will protect my family." Half the time, we're not even conscious wishful thinking. It is like putting a bandage over our fears that allows us to get on with our day-to-day life or imagine that everything will be better at some mythical point in the future.

"When I was twenty, my first boyfriend was thirty-two,"

explained Craig who was forty when he started coming to see me for counseling. "He had his own business, good car and a nice home. He was an adult and I was floundering about trying to work out who I was and what I was going to be. So for years, I had this figure of thirty-two in my head as the time when I would be grownup and feel comfortable in my own skin."

Except thirty-two had come and gone and Craig still did not feel sure of himself. Instead of using wishful thinking—that someday by osmosis or simply by being older his relationship with himself would improve—he was ready to do the hard work of challenging the unhelpful (and often homophobic) messages from his childhood and truly come to terms with being gay.

Downside at middle age

Although wishful thinking, especially when combined with magical and heroic thinking, can keep the show on the road, there comes a point when events pile up one on top of another and we can no longer ignore the evidence of our own eyes. It normally happens somewhere in our forties or fifties.

Peter, forty-eight, had used one of the most common forms of wishful thinking: "If I make everybody else happy then I'll be happy or they'll make me happy." He hadn't actually articulated this piece of wishful thinking to himself but it was clear from our first session:

"I've worked my butt off for years for my wife and kids and what thanks do I get?" he said. "I have to work away from home because that's how I earn enough to afford their expensive private schools. Have you any idea what it's like to come back to an empty hotel room at the end of a long day? Soulless. When I finally come home, they're completely wrapped up in texting, skyping, or whatever with their mates. My wife tells me not to get 'bent out of shape' by it because that's what teenagers do. So I'm in the wrong again."

"So you're a people-pleaser, you want to be liked and make everybody else happy," I suggested. "You're so tuned into what other people want, you don't really know what you need."

The greatest problem of being a people-pleaser, and wishful thinking in general, is that you can end up going down a path that other people approve of but that doesn't fulfill *you*. No wonder so many people in middle age feel lost and disappointed.

Like many people in this situation, Peter blamed his wife for holding him back—but the picture is always far more complicated than we imagine. (I will look into the wider influences in a moment, but first I have an exercise to help you take stock of the different developmental stages.)

EXERCISE LIFE GRAPH

In order to draw an overview of your life to date, I'd like you to chart your ups and downs. Look at the graph below, starting from the baseline with your earliest memories (whenever that might be), through the years to today. Draw a line showing which periods were good times and which were bad. Afterward, mark the events or situations that brought about the peaks and troughs.

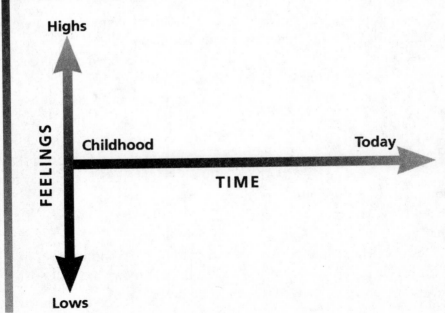

40

Finally, consider the following questions:

1. What is the balance between your good and bad times?

2. Are there any patterns that stand out?

3. Have you spent a lot of time around the baseline (with nothing really high or low) or do you swing from one extreme to another? If either of these situations apply, why do you think this might be?

4. What has surprised you from doing this exercise?

5. How does putting your current dilemmas into the context of your whole life change your outlook on them?

THE WIDER INFLUENCES

When you finally stop using magical and heroic thinking and take off the wishful-thinking glasses, you can begin to take stock of your life and ask yourself: How did I get here? However, it's harder to answer this question than you might imagine. There's a whole host of influences about how to live that you don't really notice because they are so all encompassing. Some of the messages are so strong that they don't have to be said or the instructions have been given so often that you've taken them on board without actually questioning their validity.

Parents

Children want to be accepted and loved, so they strive to please and learn what will make their parents happy, but equally they fear disapproval and even abandonment. The result is that they develop finely tuned antennae to work out what their parents want or think is right.

"My strongest memory as a child was taking my father to the rail station every Monday morning," Peter told me. "I used to be devastated that I wouldn't be seeing him until Friday evening and in floods of tears. As I grew older, I learnt to control my tears because it upset my mother, but I never accepted the idea that he'd be away all week."

"Did you question why he had to work away?" I asked.

"I knew he didn't really like it because he always said how much he missed us."

"So you learnt two things as a child. First, men provide for their family, no matter what the cost to themselves. Second, in your family, everybody got on with what was expected of them without complaint. Your father accepted working away, your mother accepted being the sole parent during the week, and you accepted not 'making a fuss' at the station."

"Although I vowed not to fall into the same trap, I've copied my father," said Peter. "I work away during the week and I don't complain even though it makes me miserable."

"So the unspoken rules in your family were 'keep your head down' and 'don't make a fuss' and 'men provide?'"

These messages had been so much part of the air that Peter had breathed as a child that he had never stopped to ask himself if there were alternatives. What would happen if you did make a fuss? Was there more to life as an adult than paying the bills? Could he become more than a provider? He certainly felt that his job as a loss adjuster no longer defined him and I saw a sensitive and complex man who felt things deeply—rather the stereotypical stoic that he'd been taught would prosper in the wider world.

Many of my clients realize at middle age that they are still trying to please their parents. Even if they have rebelled and done something different, their life has still been framed by their parents' beliefs.

Katrina, fifty-three, was a dentist, although since becoming a mother she practiced part-time. Her father had been a doctor, a senior consultant at an important teaching hospital, and Katrina and her two brothers were brought up to study hard and succeed. (They were the first generation of their family to be born into the UK; both their father and mother had arrived in the country with little more than the clothes they stood up in.)

"The only thing that mattered in our family was medicine," explained Katrina. "I remember once my father caught me writing a story and he told me, 'That's all well and good but you should be studying.'"

Although all three children did well at school, "My father is only really interested in my youngest brother who became a doctor—even though my other brother became a lawyer. You'd think dentistry was a sort of medicine but somehow that doesn't count."

At the next counseling session, Katrina reported going home to visit her father and how it had encouraged her to look at her life through fresh eyes.

"I thought I was striking out on my own by choosing to be a dentist but I've never really escaped the shadow of his expectations or stopped trying to make him proud. My father never really took me seriously and I think that's why I have to keep proving myself, why everything has to be perfect but, of course, it can't be, so I lose my temper with myself, my husband, and my children."

Remember Joseph Campbell's idea that it is harder to transition into an adult today as our society has no initiation ceremonies? It got me thinking: what instructions might our distant ancestors have given round the campfire? They would have told stories (because that's the best way to instil a child with the myths and legends of a society). We still have storytelling in the form of folk tales, and we're still telling them to our children (as bedtime stories and in movies).

Robert Bly is an American poet and leader of the American mythopoetic movement (which aims to liberate men from the constraints of the modern world and put them in touch with their true masculine nature). He takes one of the *Grimm's Fairy Tales,* "Iron John," and deconstructs it.

In the story, there is a wild and dangerous man (Iron John) locked in an iron cage in the courtyard of the castle, and a young prince (our hero) with a golden ball. The boy prince has been given strict instructions by his father (the king) not to talk to Iron John but one day, while he's playing, the golden ball rolls into Iron John's cage and the wild man grabs it. The prince wants his ball back but Iron John refuses unless the prince unlocks the door to the cage (but the king has forbade anyone on pain of death, to set him free). At first the boy refuses to listen to Iron John, but he wants his ball back, so the next day he returns to the cage and tries to negotiate. Iron John tells him that the key is under his mother's pillow. I expect you can guess what happens next. When the king is out hunting, the boy steals the key and releases Iron John. Next, he climbs onto the wild man's back and goes off with him into the forest.

The story is about coming of age and how we need to rebel against the rules of our fathers to become adults, but the interesting part is that the key is under the queen's pillow. Some people have interpreted the story with a sexual overtone but I think Bly is correct to interpret the pillow as where the mother dreams, and how her unspoken aspirations for the boy are just as powerful (if not more so) than the father's explicit instructions to his son.

Although Robert Bly's *Iron John: A book about men* (Addison-Wesley, 1990) interprets the story of adolescence for boys, girls have to make the same journey and unite with the parts of their personality that have been deemed less valuable by their parents in order to become women, too. Bly writes:

"The possessiveness that mothers typically exercise on sons—not to mention the possessiveness that fathers typically exercise on daughters—can never be underestimated."

Society

The messages from our wider society are probably even more powerful than those from our parents because, after all, our father and mother are ingesting society's dominant values and reinforcing them by repeating them back to us. So what are these messages? Once again, we take them so much at face value that we neither question them nor realize how deeply they impact on our lives, nor understand how much we use them to measure our own values. It's a bit like asking: do fish know that they are swimming in water?

Paul Verhaeghe is a professor of psychoanalysis at the University of Ghent in Belgium and author of *What About Me? The struggle for identity in a market-based society* (Scribe, 2014). He believes that our culture and identity used to be determined by four competing areas: religion, politics, arts, and the economy. From 1979 onward, what he refers to as the neoliberal view of humanity began to dominate. He summarizes it as follows:

"People are competitive beings focused on their own profit. This benefits society as a whole because competition entails everyone doing their best to come out on top. As a result, we get better and cheaper products and more efficient services within a single free market, unhampered by government. This is ethically right because success or failure in that competition depends entirely on individual effort." (Taken from *What About Me? The Struggle for Identity in a Market-based Society,* Paul Verhaeghe, published by Scribe UK, 2014. Reproduced with permission.)

So the market and profit has triumphed over all else and the message is clear: we must continue to improve ourselves because the competition is fierce. The idea of social progress from the Enlightenment onward has moved away from creating a better society (or attaining a utopia) into the perfectible individual. What counts most is being financially successful and that is measured by visible wealth, the quality of our possessions, and our social status. No wonder we fear failure so much and find it hard to tolerate the smallest setback.

With our relationship to the economy being the primary way of defining our value, how does this affect how we understand ourselves, particularly when we are in our forties and fifties and realizing the truth behind the notion from American philosopher William James (1842–1910): "The exclusive worship of the bitch-goddess success is our national disease?"

Society used to be deeply religious and faith framed our day-to-day life. So the question "Am I leading my life properly?"—a key issue in the middle passage—would have been considered in respect to whether we were fulfilling God's purpose for us. Even though religion was already less important when I was growing up in the sixties and seventies, I was still given some basic knowledge about the Bible and the Christian calendar at school. A study of 2,000 parents in 2015 found that 79% of children did not know the reason for the Easter celebration. A quarter thought it celebrated the birthday of the Easter Bunny and even more thought it marked the invention of chocolate. Tellingly, the survey was not commissioned by a university or a religious organization but a chain of hotels seeking to link their brand name with family Easter breaks. No wonder that religion in the West today hardly dents the supremacy of the financial markets.

Art used to be about truth, beauty, and insights into how to live, or it provided a different window onto the world. It would take time and the judgment of successive generations to decide if a painting, play, or book had any merit. For example, Jane Austen (1775–1817) had little fame in her lifetime, received few positive reviews, and did not become wealthy from her writing. By the mid-nineteenth century she was admired by the literary elite but it wasn't until her nephew's memoir, published in 1870, that her books became available in popularly priced editions, and not until the 1940s that she was widely accepted as a great novelist. Nowadays the Internet has effectively removed the gatekeepers—editors, curators, and critics—so everybody can self-publish their books or distribute their art or their opinions on social media (and become widely followed and therefore important and ultimately financially successful). Art is judged by sales, box office rankings, and chart positions or alternatively the number of awards won. The most talked-about book of 2014 was by Zoella, a video blogger (or vlogger), who broke all records as the fastest-selling debut novelist since records began (78,109 copies in one week) but was later revealed not to have actually written her novel *Girl Online*.

This focus on the number of units sold can make it harder to find the underlying truth and beauty in art. I have been drawn to art galleries in times of personal crisis, but it is only now that I realize I was really looking for mystery and transcendence. In other words, I was trying to engage with a central challenge of the middle passage: what gives life meaning?

Politics has also downgraded its own reference points. It is no longer the struggle between two overarching global ideologies, capitalism and socialism, but a bid for who can manage the economy the best. The job of the state is not to provide for citizens but to step out of the way and let business become more efficient and individuals consume. Politicians are widely despised, considered to be in the pockets of big business, and mainly the fodder for stand-up comedians. If politicians seem impotent, it can make the rest of us feel even more vulnerable.

So what is the impact of neoliberal thinking on our self-esteem and, in particular, what it means to be forty- or fifty-something? First, with the relentless emphasis on success, the number of winners is, by definition, limited, and you are only as good as your last performance review or set of sales figures. Second, the rise of constant evaluation (inherent in defining success) in workplaces encourages people to adapt to some empty scoring system. And finally, there is a stripping away of diversity as power is centralized and each individual has less and less say over how their work is done. This can lead to a crisis of confidence at any age but it is particularly telling in the middle passage when we are focused on what makes life (and our work) meaningful.

Children

Raising the next generation is one of the most satisfying roles on offer today. So for many people, being a mother or father is at the heart of their identity. And yet, there's a problem with over-identifying with any role—whether it is your job, being a great partner, or the best parent possible. Instead of coming from the inside, your sense of self-worth is tied to forces outside your control. Your employer could be taken over by another company and your job may disappear in the restructuring. As I discovered, your partner can fall ill and die. And your children *will* grow up, become teenagers who need you less, hopefully go off to university and, one day, leave home altogether.

Jane, forty-two, had a part-time job teaching badminton but her main focus was her three children: her sons of sixteen and ten, and her daughter of fourteen. When they were younger, they really needed her. Now the oldest two were teenagers asserting their independence, and she was aware that her "baby" was growing up too.

"I'm beginning to question, what is my purpose in life? At the school gates I'm known as Anton, Sasha, or Pier's mommy, but surely I'm more than that. Up until now, I haven't had time to even think about such complex questions because there's always something to keep me busy."

It's not just that you're no longer the center of your children's life —or that they are moody and withdrawn—but they are beginning to think "Who am I?" and "What am I going to do with my life?" themselves. Time and again, when I consider why a crisis in a relationship is happening now, I find that a teenager going through an identity crisis has triggered something similar in my client.

Jane did not go through the traditional teenage rebellion because her parents divorced when she was twelve and she had been too busy supporting her mother and trying to keep at least the semblance of peace with her father.

"I would edit any of the pleasures out of my day with Dad because it would prompt a lecture from Mom about him being 'free and easy' and 'buying my love.' The strain at home meant that I became a bit of a dreamer, and I would fall into a trance in class. When my grades slipped, even though it was only slightly because I was a good girl who worked hard, my father went into overdrive and sent long lists of instructions to my mother about how I should study and when. These notes made my mother so angry that I would deliberately lose them."

With Jane's main focus on pleasing each parent, she had no time for the usual teenager introspection, and if she had stopped to think about what she wanted, she would have probably come up with something like "to not be like my parents" or "to not put my children through what I went through." (These are fine aims—and a great starting point—but being the opposite of your parents is not a well-rounded identity.) Unsurprisingly, her own children becoming teenagers triggered an identity crisis for her. She found any challenge from her own children especially wounding (because she had never behaved like that to her parents) and any argument felt like a catastrophe rather than an inevitable part of living with teenagers (because being a mother was the center of her life, rather than just one of a number of roles, and "good" mothers don't scream at their children).

If your children have been at the center of your life, it can be harder to answer the central question of the middle passage: who am I? (beyond the sum of my roles) and the follow-on question: so what am I going to do with the rest of my life?

Peers

As I have discussed, our identity is bound up with the people closest to us. We are the child of, the partner of, the parent of, or the sibling of somebody. There is also a wider circle that is equally important. Our professional identity is tied up with our relationship with our colleagues and the messages they give us. If you are the homemaker, your identity will be centered on how well your children are doing (or to be more accurate, their grades and exam results and network of friendships) and how you measure up to the other mothers or fathers at the school gates.

We have always compared our success, our happiness, and our self-worth against these peers—along with our friends and our contemporaries—but the advent of social media and reality TV means that we are comparing ourselves with a much wider pool.

Twitter and Instagram are full of people posing in expensive designer clothes and jewelry or inside their new sports car, and Facebook can become a contest for who has the most exciting and fulfilling life. In previous generations, the newspapers served up "poor little rich girl" stories about Woolworth heiress Barbara Hutton (1912–1979) who during the Depression was one of the world's richest women, but on her deathbed was on the verge of bankruptcy after seven husbands and countless relationships with exploitative men; or shipping heiress Christina Onassis (1950–1988) who lost all of her closest family over two and a half years and battled with her weight, depression, and prescription-drug addiction, and divorced four husbands. The message was clear: extreme wealth brings extreme unhappiness. Conversely, today's media is full of the rich and famous inviting us to marvel at their lovely homes and wonderful lifestyles. Meanwhile, reality TV offers up groups of rich show-offs from glamorous places like Beverly Hills and Chelsea or hapless individuals in undesirable locations trying to keep body and soul together on benefits or involved in borderline legal activities. The message is similarly clear: to be rich and therefore successful is virtuous and to be poor and therefore unsuccessful is a moral failing.

EXERCISE RANK THE INFLUENCES

Look at the following list of possible influences that have helped shape your identity, past and present. Beside each one I'd like you to note a favorite saying, expectation, or unspoken message from that person, institution, organization, cultural phenomenon, or role, even if it is only something minor. For example, when you were growing up what did your nationality mean to you, and what does it mean now? How important was your local community to you when you were a child, and how significant is it today?

Your mother _____

Your father _____

Grandparents _____

Sibling _____

School _____

Faith _____

Nationality _____

Sexuality _____

Gender _____

Favorite TV show _____

Hobby _____

Family _____

Local community _____

Nationality _____

Race _____

Work colleague_____

Classmate _____

Favorite book growing up _____

Sport _____

Career _____

University/further education _____

Being a parent _____

Political allegiance _____

Partner_____

Include any other significant influence that does not fit under any of the headings above. Next, rank your influences in descending order of importance. Finally, are there any messages that you would like to challenge or consider out of date?

WHO FINDS THE MIDDLE PASSAGE PARTICULARLY PROBLEMATIC?

I've yet to meet anyone who doesn't find the challenges of getting older difficult, but there are three types of people who are more likely to have a crisis in their forties and fifties. I call these the good child, the golden child, and the lost child. Although all three groups have used magical, heroic, and wishful thinking to keep the show on the road and be a "success"; each one has a signature approach and the loss of it can be particularly devastating.

Good child

Children have an amazing ability to respond intuitively to their parents, to please them, and to fulfill their needs. The good child is not only well-behaved but good at playing the assigned role—for example: confidant, comforter, adviser, ally, carer of younger siblings etc. Instead of the principal caregiver supporting and accepting the feelings of the child, the roles are reversed and the good child is focused on preserving the equilibrium of the parents (and thereby securing their love). So if a parent is suppressing unacceptable feelings like jealousy, anger, helplessness, pain, or neediness, the child will do the same. Equally if a parent is exposing a small child to a significant level of strong feelings—like anxiety or depression—the son or daughter will seek to balance out the atmosphere and suppress their own fears or unhappiness (for fear of making their principal carer feel worse and risk losing their love).

I always know when I have a good child in my counseling room because they are particularly respectful of authority figures (ie. a stand-in parent like me) and take every word I say as gospel (handed down on tablets of stone). If I give them homework—doing a practical exercise or asking them to get hold of a book—they are extremely conscientious and hand in ten times more notes than I expect, or they have read most of the book by the next time we meet. These good children might seem the ideal client (and that's certainly what they are aiming for) but as my goal is to encourage them to be their authentic selves, it can take a lot of challenging and permission-giving before they are able to do what is right for them (rather than what they think I want).

Justine, forty-one, felt that her mother had "downloaded" her personality into her. So I asked her to list some of the messages that she believed she had received from her mother. I was not surprised when the first one was "to be good." So what were the others?

"I needed to fulfill her expectations and live the life she didn't have—because she got married at twenty and had her first child at twenty-two," she told me. "Although she didn't actually say that she wanted me to be a high flyer and earn good money, she certainly wanted more money herself. In the summer vacation, I worked for a market-gardening business and I was really interested in the science of plants but I knew that would never pay really well. So I went into sales."

Justine had become successful and headed a team covering Europe and North America.

"What's it like being a good child?" I asked her.

"I don't think I was allowed to grow up and I still want to please everybody like my bosses and my husband to the most unhealthy level," she replied. "He's not certain whether he wants children or not, so I haven't pushed it because I don't want to rock the boat. So I'm left at forty-one, running out of time, and not certain whether I could cope with upsetting my husband."

Another client, Philip, forty-five, had an insecure mother who needed constant reassurance. "When we went away on school summer camp, the other boys wouldn't phone their mothers even once. They'd be too busy helping build a fire or exploring the woods. I'd be in the queue for the phone box with all the nice girls and my mother would be in tears and make me feel guilty for going away. Even though I never missed a night, she still needed to hear how much I missed home, her home cooking and, of course, her too. I used to edit all the dangerous and exciting events out of my 'what we did today' speech as that could upset her and promote a barrage of 'be careful' and 'do you think that's a good idea?'"

On a superficial level, good children make good partners because they are always seeking to please and therefore routinely put themselves second. In some cases, they don't know what they want because they've been so focused on others' needs. Good children also use bucketloads of **wishful thinking** to preserve their own equilibrium—in particular: "If I make everybody else happy, they will make me happy" or "Making other people happy makes me happy." However, when faced with the reality of how life really is—rather than how they wish it would be—these good children/partners are capable of acts of extraordinary selfishness. Instead of learning how to tune into their own needs and express them clearly to their partner, they can withdraw, become angry, and act out their unhappiness by flirting with a colleague or starting an affair. Instead of learning that caring for others is only fulfilling if you also look after yourself, they can easily slide into depression.

Golden child

My counseling practice is full of golden children who were praised for their talents, appreciated for their achievements, and made their parents proud. In most cases, they were "good" children but they received a second, even stronger message: be successful. So while the good children feared losing their parents' love if they were uncooperative, golden children only felt admired for their talent, cleverness, or beauty, rather than themselves.

Mark, forty-four, can clearly remember a particularly telling conversation with his mother when he was thirteen. "My mother stressed the importance of shining bright. She didn't explain what she meant or how I should I achieve this but I took it as 'be very good at something' and then I would be valued."

Fortunately Mark did well at school, went to a leading university, and had a golden academic career. Like all golden children, he used **heroic thinking** to stave off any doubts and never once questioned whether a good degree would automatically lead to a successful career, happiness, and fulfillment. While in his early twenties, the idea that he could be anything he set his heart on was comforting and provided the courage to set up a successful business in his thirties. However, by the time he turned fifty, he had gathered enough experience of the way the world is (rather than how we want it to be) to question whether he would ever shine bright enough.

"My business is doing OK but not generating anywhere near as much money as it should be and no matter what I do, I can't seem to shift it up to the next level. I want to find a loving relationship and settle down, but despite women always complaining that they can't find a man who will commit, I'm still single," he told me.

Lots of my clients complain that life is difficult and full of suffering. They have my complete sympathy and understanding—not just because I try and empathize but because it is demonstrably true (and the first of the four noble truths on which Buddhism is based). But they often brush aside my compassion because they say they *used* to find everything easy. Perhaps they were near the top of the class without putting in too much effort, excelled at sport, or got the lead roles in school plays. University was reasonably straightforward, despite the greater competition from brighter peers, because what they needed to do to get a first-class honors degree was clearly laid out. Finding the first job in their chosen profession was harder, but there are often multiple entry points. However, with each rung up the career ladder, it becomes harder to be successful—there can only be a certain number of managers or senior partners or chief executives. When golden children come up against an obstacle—like not getting a promotion or winning a contract—they can plunge into despair.

I once interviewed legendary theater producer Thelma Holt for a newspaper article. She has countless honorary degrees and awards including an Olivier for Outstanding Achievement in 1987 and a CBE in 1994. She told me about her struggle to find the right balance of self-confidence:

"I was spoilt rotten as a child and my father died when I was very small so my mother overcompensated. When I went to RADA that was the first real world I ever saw; it had not occurred to me for one second that everywhere I went they wouldn't be thrilled to have me. I came down to London thinking I was 24-carat gold and soon found out that I wasn't. But I'm not 9-carat, I'm 18-carat. I am right to be aware of my own worth because I can immediately recognize talent in others. If you don't think you have any skills, you can't recognize them in anyone else."

These are hard lessons to learn at any age but particularly difficult when you're middle-aged, with younger competitors coming up behind you and time apparently running out ahead of you.

Lost child

Although most people report a happy childhood, it is not the case for a significant proportion of my clients. Between 4 and 7% of children lose a parent and the effect on the remaining parent may mean that the child doesn't properly grieve the loss until the middle passage, until they reach the age of their mother or father when he or she died, or when their other parent dies. Sometimes it takes only a few questions to reveal a level of neglect from parents that wouldn't be out of place in a Dickens novel—while other people offer excuses for their parents' neglect or even abuse. Whether someone acknowledges that they had a traumatic childhood or not, the impact is the same. If their feelings were not taken seriously or accepted as a child, they don't have a secure enough foundation from which to explore the world or a clear enough sense of who they are as adults. I call this group the lost children.

Martin, fifty-three, had been regularly beaten by his stepfather and his mother had been too afraid to protect her son. She would regularly encourage him to be brave and he couldn't express his anger, pain, or unhappiness for fear of making her anxious that he was, in her words, "rocking the boat." It is difficult being a small child in a world of big adults who control everything. But you have one advantage: plenty of time.

"I couldn't wait to be old enough to leave home and find a better world," he told me. "I knew it had to be there. I saw it on the TV and caught glimpses into the lives of other boys at school. Although, I couldn't have real friends because I couldn't bring anyone home and nobody could know what was going on."

The coping strategy used by lost children is **magical thinking**, which kept them afloat when they were small.

"We lived on the coast and I once found a one-dollar note on the beach," said Martin. "I must have been about seven or eight. I gave it to my mother for 'running away' money. I don't know whether she saved it or spent it but she was immensely pleased. I lived in hope that one day I'd find a life-changing amount. Other children had their heads in the clouds but I was always looking at my feet."

To paraphrase the Swiss psychologist Alice Miller (1923–2010), who was an expert on parental neglect and psychological abuse and author of the classic book *The Drama of Being a Child* (first published in English in 1981): "the deeper the hole in the heart, the bigger the jewels in the crown need to be." In other words, the pain is so big that the distractions need to become larger and larger.

Martin tried smoking (two packets a day by eighteen), then gambling and finally cocaine: "Although I would feel momentarily better, my life descended into chaos and I became an addict." Only magical thinking would have provided the hope that any of those substances could fill the hole in his heart.

As I explained in chapter one, one of the main tasks of the middle passage is to deal with issues that have been patched up or ignored in the past. This is particularly difficult for lost children because the pain is so great, the events long ago and some of the key people are dead or frail. The risk is that they will try to soldier on and either increase their distractions or slide into depression.

SUMMING UP

➤ There are three types of childhood and provisional adult thinking—magical, heroic, and wishful—that help us through the first part of our lives. If we are overly dependent on them in our middle years, they can easily tip us into crisis.

➤ Whereas meaning used to be derived from religion, art, politics, and the economy, the triumph of neoliberal thinking has placed all the emphasis on winning, success, and money.

➤ Without realizing it, you could be leading the life that your parents or society believes is right for you.

CHAPTER THREE

Dealing with depression

Without the help of magical, heroic, and wishful thinking, the world can look bleak. Perhaps your work, which used to be meaningful to you, has become more about meeting targets. You've reached an age when you're finally beginning to think for yourself but now you feel infantilized by central office who use technology and top-down reorganization that has taken away your autonomy. Perhaps your relationship has become characterized by domesticity, duty, and maybe even drudgery? What happened to the special connection with your partner and the spark that made you feel alive? Perhaps your children are going through the moody, ungrateful, and angry stage or are about to leave home. Meanwhile, your friends are beginning to die of cancer, brain tumors, or heart attacks. It's enough to make anybody feel depressed.

I expect you've been nodding your head all the way through that last paragraph, but what I'm going to say next may come as a shock: it's OK to feel depressed (and maybe it's even good to be depressed)! I know this goes against everything our society believes in and if you've been depressed (or are currently) you will know how debilitating it can be. However, there is a big difference between feeling depressed and undiagnosed clinical depression—and if you feel you might be suffering from the latter, you need to book an appointment with your doctor.

EXERCISE WHAT ARE FEELINGS?

The purpose of this exercise and how it will help you to navigate the U-shaped life will become clear as you work your way through this chapter. Right now, I want your immediate top of your head response. Look at the following statement and find three different ways of completing this sentence:

Feelings are ...

Feelings are ...

Feelings are ...

And now I'd like you to answer these questions:

1. Which is the most accurate definition for you?

2. How would your mother have completed the sentence? (I'm interested in the mother from when you were a child, not how she might answer today.)

3. How would your father have completed the sentence? (If you didn't know your father well, imagine how he might have answered using what knowledge you have.)

4. What impact have these beliefs about feelings had on your life? (If you can't answer this question yet, come back to it when you've finished the chapter.)

THE WISDOM OF DEPRESSION

It is a startling combination: depression and wisdom. How could you learn anything from something as miserable and potentially life-destroying as depression? It's a good question. To help me explain, I want to go over the response to this exercise from William, a 48-year-old lawyer, as they reflect a quite common view. He wrote:

Feelings are not something we did in our family
Feelings are dangerous

Feelings are divided up into good ones (which you want more of) and bad ones (which are best avoided or got through as quickly as possible).

I asked him how his mother would have responded.

"When I was a teenager, she was worried that I'd get too involved with a girl, be love-stuck, and distracted from my school work. So, she would say something like *feelings are bad for your grades,*" William replied.

How about his father?

"He was a bit of a mystery wrapped up in an enigma. So he would say something like *feelings are something you keep secret* or *feelings are unknowable.*"

So which of William's definitions was the most important to him?

"I suppose it has to be *feelings are dangerous* and therefore need to be controlled."

At this point, I'd like to share what I consider feelings to be. I hasten to add that this is just my opinion and there are plenty of other valid answers. I believe that *feelings are clues about how to react or behave.* Therefore if you're feeling depressed, it could be for a very good reason. For example, you're facing what seems an insurmountable problem or are feeling worn down by life. In other words, depressed feelings can be a natural and healthy response to feeling stuck, taken advantage of, or unappreciated. When you're depressed, you lack energy and want to slow down; instead of being the life and soul of the party, you prefer to be quiet and withdraw into yourself. Guess what? Silence and contemplation are really positive ways for pinpointing a problem and thereby starting to resolve it. We might not like the circumstances that tip us into feeling depressed but in the words of Meister Eckhart (1260–1328), a German philosopher and theologian, "Truly, it's in the darkness that one finds the light, so when we are in sorrow then the light is nearest of all to us."

Unfortunately, we live in a culture that doesn't believe in stopping and reflecting (flu is for wimps) and gives men unhelpful messages (don't show weakness) and expects so much from woman (be an earth mother and have a successful career). We were brought up in families that had often ambivalent attitudes to emotions. (In mine the message was "discussing problems only makes them worse." No surprise I became a therapist!) Therefore, it is difficult to trust our natural responses if they are painful or disorientating.

If, despite these pressures, you stop and begin to think through your problems, they can seem overwhelming. The possible solutions could hurt those nearest to us, seem unworkable, or just too hard. The temptation is stop contemplating before you've really started (and therefore not looked past the surface problems) or had the chance to become truly creative (and research possible solutions).

Shutting down is a workable strategy in the short-term. But if you repeatedly turn down the invitation for renewal offered by depressed feelings and distract yourself, minimizing the problem or gritting your teeth and keeping going, you risk tipping over from feeling depressed (a natural and healthy response) into clinical depression (a major depression that is considered by the medical profession to be an illness).

WHAT HAPPENS IF YOU DON'T LISTEN TO YOUR FEELINGS?

In the UK, 23.5 million days were lost due to work-related ill health in 2013/14 (according to the Health and Safety Executive), of which mental-health issues accounted for just over half the figure—with the average time off for stress, depression, or anxiety being twenty-three days. Although these statistics are alarming enough, they hide an epidemic of undiagnosed depression that falls into three categories.

Low-level depression

For many people with low-level depression, feeling down is such an everyday part of their lives that it can feel more about their character—and the world around them—than a response to particular circumstances. Therefore it is not surprising that the majority of suf-ferers have not discussed the problem with the doctor and—in some cases—not even their family or friends. They just accept it as part of their lot. If they did seek professional help, they could be diagnosed as having dysthymia (from the Ancient Greek meaning "bad state of mind"). It is considered less severe than clinical depression but longer-lasting. Here are some of the indicators:

- Are you eating too much or too little?

- Are you finding it hard to sleep or sleeping too much?

- Do you feel tired or lacking in energy for most of the day?

- Do you suffer from low self-esteem or feel inadequate most of the time?

- Do you have trouble concentrating or making decisions?

- Do you feel hopeless or pessimistic about the future?

If you answered yes to two or more questions and you've been feeling this way for more than two years, you could be suffering from dysthymia and should seek professional advice.

Genevieve, thirty-seven, started counseling partly because she was finding it hard to form long-term relationships but mainly because she was unhappy in general: "Perhaps it's been going on for twelve years but it's so much part of me that it's become the status quo. I feel like a chair with four wobbly legs."

I found it an interesting metaphor and asked her to expand it.

"My job is not fulfilling—that's the first wobble. There's also a general lack of meaning in my life; my social life and relationships with friends is OK, but like everybody else in London we're so busy that it seems impossible to meet up. I suppose the fourth wobbly leg is a general lack of balance."

Like a lot of people with low-level depression, there had been times when it had tipped over into a major depressive episode. The first had occurred at university (she was the first member of her family to go into higher education) when student life had failed to live up to her expectations and Genevieve became anxious about her future after graduation. The second episode was in her late thirties after her brother died. On both occasions, Genevieve had cognitive-behavioral therapy (more about this treatment later) and although her mood lifted, the background grayness never quite went away.

What is the impact? It is very easy to slip down the "exhaustion funnel"—a term coined by Professor Marie Asberg at the Karolinska Institute in Stockholm, Sweden. Sleep problems bring about a lack of energy, aches and pains, and guilt about your performance (both at home and work). Next comes a sense of joylessness and feeling depressed. The final destination is exhaustion.

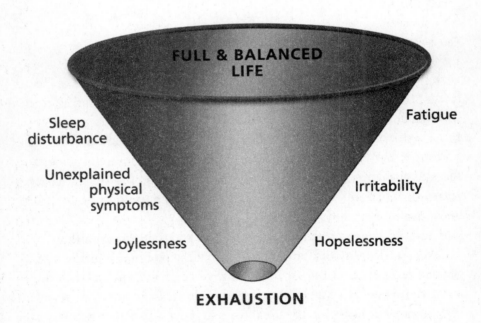

As you slide down the funnel, you give up more activities that nourish you—like your hobbies and seeing friends—because you're tired, underperforming, and need to knuckle down. The result is that your life is increasingly dominated by work and chores and responsibility (activities that can starve you of joy).

Low-level depression can also exaggerate your personality so that you can become a caricature of yourself. If you are angry, you will be angrier. If you are critical (of yourself and others), the criticism will be magnified and your patience reduced. If you are dutiful and responsible, you will become even more obsessed with getting things done and have even less time for fun.

It is little wonder that Genevieve felt unbalanced and rundown.

Avoided depression

If you were to meet someone with avoided depression at a party, you would probably never guess what was going on beneath the surface. They have a good job or they are creative and full of ideas for new projects. They smile and joke a lot, so it's only when you've left the party that you might reflect that some of the conversation was rather dark or conversely they went out of their way to convince you that everything was wonderful in their life.

When I quizzed Justine from the previous chapter about how her mother downloaded her personality into her, she told a story with a broad grin on her face about being spanked in public.

"We'd be shopping in some department store and for a child it seemed she'd been in there forever. So I'd get bored and start poking the merchandise—not doing any damage or anything—and she'd warn me to stop, but there would be a devil inside me and I'd touch the roll of fabric (or whatever) again and she'd take down my knickers and spank me in the store. My brothers and sisters would get the same treatment. We often tell the story and laugh."

"I don't find the story funny and I wonder why you're smiling," I reflected back. "What other feelings could be around?"

"I suppose it's rather sad," admitted Justine.

"That's exactly what I was thinking because you were a 'good' child—always trying to please her."

"And it was terribly humiliating. She never spanked us at home."

While I felt sad for the little girl she had been, Justine was feeling sad for her mother: "She was so insecure and worried that our bad behavior would reflect on her."

"So you feel sorry for your mother rather than the younger version of yourself: why do you think that might be?"

It was like a light bulb had gone on.

"If I was sorry for myself, it would be overwhelming," she said. "I was depressed when I was twelve and I'd be sobbing so uncontrollably in the classroom that I'd be sent into the corridor with my face turned to the wall. I don't want to go back there again."

So, as with most cases of avoided depression, the deep distress had been denied and pushed away for fear that if the depression came to the surface it would be impossible to escape.

What is the impact? If you are avoiding depression, you will need to do more than "put on a happy face" or "look on the bright side" to ward off sadness. The most common defenses against depression are striving to be perfect, successful, and grandosity. I use the last term in the general sense: grand in an imposing or impressive way. However, in psychiatry, over the past twenty-five years, it has changed from having an exaggerated belief in one's abilities (a trap into which most of us can fall) into a symptom of a narcissistic personality disorder or being bipolar (which are much rarer conditions).

If you were admired as a child for being good or golden, you will have made a link between being admired and being loved. It is important to excel in everything and your self-respect depends on it. When your powers fail (maybe because you're getting older, feel burned out, or the law of averages means you just can't succeed in every project), you risk falling into depression unless you try harder still with ever-increasing displays of brilliance.

In some ways, depression and grandiosity are two sides of the same coin. So what have they got in common?

■ Fragile self-esteem.

■ Negative internal voices.

- Perfectionism.

- A false self is presented to the world (because there's no strong sense of who you are behind the mask, or you're too busy pleasing others and trying to be loved).

- Lack of confidence in your own feelings and wishes.

- Fear of loss, so great readiness to conform.

- Oversensitivity—especially to guilt and shame.

- Unacknowledged anger.

- Restlessness.

Unfortunately, human beings are not perfect and nobody's life is a series of unparalleled successes and—particularly in the middle passage when we are being called to be authentic—it is easy for mild grandiosity to tip into depression. The alternative, the need for success at any cost (because the fear of depression is so great) can turn into narcissism (total disregard for the feelings of others) or even trigger a bipolar disorder (abnormally happy and energetic phases alternating with the blackest depression where it becomes impossible to function normally).

Unresolved depression

While it is possible for the nearest and dearest of those people with low-level depression or avoided depression to be unaware of their condition, unresolved depression is often obvious to everybody except for the person struggling with it. In some cases, the sufferer will be in complete denial: "I'm stressed. Everybody gets stressed. When I finish this project, everything will be back to normal." It is equally common for the sufferer to realize there's a problem but refuse all help: "I can do this on my own" or "I've read a couple of inspirational blogs, I know what I need to do."

If this is you, I am torn between admiration for your courage and concern. It is possible to tough out low-level depression (which may eventually pass), but it is harder to face down ingrained clinical depression. As the levels of pain and unhappiness increase—because ignored problems seldom get better on their own—you need stronger relief. So while your coping strategies might start at the positive end (for example, going for a run or taking a long bath) they can quickly move into more dangerous territory (for example, alcohol, cocaine, gambling). Most of us have no problem enjoying a drink to unwind, but without really realizing what is happening you can move from enjoying to needing alcohol. Instead of tackling the underlying depression (and the problems behind it), you start self-medicating. Once again, this short-term strategy can manage the sadness but, all too often, what was a crutch to support you turns into a stick to beat yourself.

Oscar, forty-five, was a successful city lawyer with deep-seated unresolved depression. Unfortunately, this was not the reason why he and his wife, Jackie, forty-two, consulted me. He had had a short-term affair with a junior college and although he stopped the affair and tried to arrange for her to be transferred to another team, his wife was still distraught and he felt under immense pressure. Their arguments were going round and round in circles.

"I understand that I have to prove that I'm trustworthy and be home at a reasonable time, but Jackie doesn't understand that I have to socialize with clients after work and I can't always drop everything and come home," he said.

"But alcohol and socializing was how you and she started the affair," Jackie retorted, "and you've no idea what it's like to be sitting at home, heart in my mouth, worrying that you're not on the train that you said you'd be."

At first, I thought I needed to help Oscar and Jackie to negotiate so he would have a degree of flexibility for his work and she could feel safer. It soon became clear that Oscar had a serious drink problem and that this was a nonsubject between the couple. Oscar would get defensive and angry and Jackie would then back off to minimize the impact on her. Christmas was looming on the horizon —when corporate entertaining goes into overdrive—and I tried to help the couple to plan ahead. But Oscar was under so much stress at work and at home that one evening he drank so much at a party that he blacked out and didn't come home at all.

"I was on my way to the station in a taxi and that's the last I remember. I know it was late. Did I miss the last train? Somehow I lost my phone and I must have been wandering around because I woke up, sometime after 6 a.m., on a bench," he explained.

Fortunately, the experience had been enough of a wake-up call for him to consult his family doctor. Unfortunately, he was not prepared to seek specialist support.

"I know I need to cut down and my doctor has given me advice on sensible drinking and tips on filling up other people's glasses rather than my own," said Oscar. "So I can beat this on my own."

For a while, his drinking was more controlled and we could explore why he had had an affair.

"Work has been really tough. Now I'm a partner there's huge pressure to bring in more and more high-paying clients. After years of climbing the ladder, I've reached a plateau and I don't know if I can get any further. I'd like to find a less stressful local job—without the long the commute and a better quality of life—but we have three children at private schools and I couldn't earn enough money."

These midlife issues about what makes life meaningful were exacerbated as Oscar had long-term identity problems to resolve.

"I was a grammar-school boy but all my colleagues went to public schools, so I've always felt that I've something to prove. Jackie's father is a very successful businessman—which is fine because he's been able to help us a couple of times, but then it's not me providing for the family because she runs to Daddy," Oscar said bitterly.

"But I've always worked *and* run the house. I thought we were a team," replied Jackie.

What is the impact? Unresolved depression is like a snowball rolling down a mountain. The longer it continues to roll, the more volume and the more momentum it picks up until eventually the snowball becomes an avalanche destroying everything in its wake. As well as depression, you have to tackle one or more layers of unhelpful coping strategies (and the chaos or addictions they can bring).

Like a lot of people with unresolved depression, Oscar had grown up in a family with rigidly defined roles for men and women. His parents had unwittingly encouraged him not to feel (because they found strong emotions uncomfortable themselves) and not to think (because "you don't want to be a dreamer" and thinking might lead to breaking their injunction about making a fuss). First, he didn't listen to his feelings (and take the wisdom that can come out of depression) and second, instead of thinking deeply (to find a smarter way to work) he worked longer and longer hours. When there were financial pressures, he didn't think outside the traditional box of what it means to be a man and share the burden with his wife. In effect, he couldn't change because that would upset the status quo (and make a fuss), so he ended up slipping into low-level depression.

By middle age, he was finding it harder to be successful enough to silence his feelings of inferiority at work, even though he had a position and career many would envy. Instead of considering what gave his life real meaning—his family and children—he was trapped in his old habits of providing. With mild grandiosity and heroic thinking losing their power, he finally tipped into full clinical depression and sadly, instead of getting help, managed his depression by drinking. Alcohol lowered his inhibitions and he got a temporary feel-good boost from the affair. The excitement and flattery from his affair partner burst through the layers of gray and, for the first time in years, he actually felt something.

"I knew the affair was wrong but at least I felt human rather than a hamster on a wheel. So I told myself this was something I needed for me and didn't really think what the impact might be on Jackie or the kids," he confessed.

After the affair was discovered, Oscar was left trying to cope with even tougher emotions: guilt and shame. Once again, he fell back on his old coping mechanism—because nobody likes to think badly of themselves for too long—so he silenced his inner critical voice and his wife's distress with alcohol.

WHAT CAUSES DEPRESSION?

In my first session with new clients, I take a history of their mental health. If I find depression, I ask about possible causes but I'm surprised how few people have a narrative for why they became depressed in the first place, even if they have had professional help. Perhaps it's understandable because even experts don't agree on the root causes of depression or the best ways to help sufferers. So what chance do ordinary people have? So let me give you an overview of the key theories of depression and share my opinions, so you can construct a narrative for why you became depressed and decide on the most suitable treatment.

The easiest type of depression to understand is situational depression. After some specific trauma like bereavement, divorce, or redundancy, you have a period of feeling low, crying jags, low energy, disrupted sleep patterns, and poor appetite. For example, twenty-four hours after my partner died, I found it took all my energy just to get from the kitchen to the bathroom and then I had to sit down before I could put my contact lenses in. I had to rest between shaving and brushing my teeth. I would have bursts of energy to get through the jobs of arranging the funeral but at times I found the gentle incline from my home to the village felt harder than climbing a mountain. Although I didn't want to accept it at the time, I had situational depression. It was a natural response to my loss and slowly I learned that it was fine to tell friends when I was tired and needed to curl up on their couch for a nap.

Closely related to situational depression is posttraumatic shock, which normally occurs within days after surviving something like a natural disaster, a road traffic accident, or an assault. It brings flashbacks along with insomnia and raised anxiety levels. Once again, it's a perfectly understandable response. As for situational depression, you have been made aware of just how dangerous the world can be and how thin the veil is between everyday life and disaster. So there is a need to stop, take stock of your life, and make changes. What I often find is that the shock can bring underlying problems up to the surface. I've had clients who have questioned their marriage when their partner failed to give them enough support after the trauma. I've had others who'd been managing low-level unhappiness by going for a run but after an accident were unable to exercise, and therefore had to face the full force of their feelings.

Another way to understand depression is to take a simple medical approach. There is a lot of good research into how inherent chemical imbalances in the brain can cause depression and there are a series of drugs to help redress the problem. There are also studies that back the idea of depression running in families. In research into identical twins, it was found that if one became depressed then there was a 76% chance of the other developing clinical depression. If the identical twins are raised apart, the figure drops to 67%, which suggests that environment and learned coping strategies also play a part rather than simple genetic susceptibility.

For many cases of depression, there is no straightforward link between cause and effect. Therefore, I want to look at some of the broader possibilities. Carl Jung (1875–1961) was the founder of analytical psychotherapy and elegantly summed up his thoughts as "Neurosis is always a substitute for legitimate suffering." By neurosis, he means mild mental health problems like depression, anxiety, and obsessive behaviors. So if we ignore our suffering, the problem will not go away but pop up somewhere else in another form. For example, if I hadn't listened to my postbereavement exhaustion and taken an occasional nap on a friend's couch—but pushed myself until I dropped—I could have slipped from situational depression into clinical depression, or not left the house because I was frightened of "flaking out" on people and perhaps become agoraphobic. In this way my legitimate suffering (following my partner's death) would have been transferred into neurosis.

In some cases, the legitimate suffering goes a long way back. Alice Miller, the Swiss psychologist who we meet in the last chapter, believes it comes from our earliest childhood. In particular, how our mother experienced the expression of our needs during the first few days and weeks of our life. She writes: "It is here that the *beginning of a later tragedy* might be set." (The italics are Miller's.)

I don't put as much store on the early days and months after birth, and I believe that most mothers do a great job overall of bonding with their babies and being alert to their needs and responses. Nevertheless, as children grow older, parents have all sorts of expectations of their children—many they are only half-conscious of—which we have already discussed: to be good, to succeed in the world, and thereby prove to the parent that they were not an inadequate mother or father. So I agree wholeheartedly with Miller when she writes: "It is not a child's task to satisfy his parent's needs." But if you felt pressure when you were small and defenseless to create a version of yourself to please other people (what Miller terms a "false self" and I might describe as wearing a mask), that could certainly give rise to legitimate suffering.

There is a final school of thought about depression that is less interested in people's life experiences, circumstances, or childhood and more interested in their thought patterns. Cognitive Behavioral Therapy is a short-term talking therapy developed in the 1960s (although it is based on the ideas of stoicism, a Greek philosophy from third century BC). CBT, as it is widely known, seeks to help you manage your problems by changing the way you think and behave. Instead of dealing with past problems, it focuses on teaching how to deal with your issues of today in a more positive manner. There are forms to fill out to help you understand your thought patterns, and six specific stages that everybody goes through. (There are even interactive software programs that you can work through with minimal or no contact with a therapist.) In effect, CBT seeks to overlay an internal critical voice with a more balanced and positive outlook on the world. Ultimately, CBT practitioners believe that depression is caused by unhelpful thinking patterns.

FOUR STATEMENTS ABOUT DEPRESSION

I've given an overview of the key theories about what triggers depression, but now I'd like to turn to your state of mind and give four possible causes for any low moods you may be regularly experiencing. If you're still unclear afterward, I will discuss the opposite of depression (because sometimes looking at the antithesis can shed fresh light). So think about the four statements below, what they might mean and how they might apply to you:

1. Depression is about suppression.

2. Depression is about anger turned inward.

3. Depression is the result of having fixed outcomes.

4. Depression is being separated from your true self.

Depression = suppression

You keep busy so that you don't have time or energy to listen to your feelings and process them. You tend to rationalize your feelings away or minimize their importance. You distract yourself or self-medicate with alcohol, drugs, carbohydrates, gambling, or other addictive behaviors. On one level, these strategies make sense because who would choose to be unhappy? Unfortunately, you can't pick and choose your emotions. You might start out by suppressing anger, sadness, and guilt, but pretty soon you end up suppressing passion, joy, and love too. Ultimately, you end up with hardly any feelings—hence your general bleakness—or you need something extremely strong (for example the excitement of an affair) to register anything at all.

If this is you: if you completed the life graph in the previous chapter, it is highly likely that your trajectory didn't rise much above the baseline nor fall much below it. (Please do the feelings diary exercise at the end of this section to become more aware of your emotions, rather than just trying to control them.)

Depression = anger turned inward

When we suppress our feelings, they seldom disappear but pop up somewhere else. With anger, the upset it causes can be expressed to someone else or just sneak out in other ways. For example, our boss blows his top with us and so we shout at somebody junior to us, or maybe we're annoyed with our kids but take it out on our partner. Alternatively, legitimate anger about our relationship (perhaps the unequal division of childcare or responsibility for chores) or our career (which no longer satisfies) or getting older (and our failing powers) or the general unfairness of the world (where hard work is not always rewarded) is suppressed and comes out as sarcasm or sniping about minor issues. Most commonly, the anger becomes your internal critical voice: "Pull yourself together" and "Can't you do anything right" and "I told you so."

If this is you: focus on naming your thought patterns and challenging your assumptions. (See the exercise "Name your thought patterns" in chapter one and "What happens if you pay attention to your thoughts" later in this chapter.) Also, remember to congratulate yourself every day for all the things you are doing right in your life.

Depression = fixed outcomes

If you were pinning your hopes, let's say, on the perfect vacation to make yourself feel better, you would be depressed when it rained and spoiled your picnic or fed up if the children bickered. If you had already decided that being together was what counted and you didn't get upset when the children were difficult, you could find alternative pleasures and end up with a vacation that wasn't what you had hoped for but was still satisfying. When we hold onto a fixed outcome— "we *must* get into this exhibition today"—then we are at the mercy of circumstances and are likely to be disappointed with ourselves, other people, or the world in general.

If this is you: Buddhists consider attachment to be the cause of all unhappiness and they teach the importance of nonattachment. So if you find yourself getting angry or depressed, your feelings are probably alerting you to your expectation of a fixed outcome. As it's easier to let go of minor attachments, start with a small upset. For example, you're stuck in a queue and getting impatient. Start by identifying your fixed outcome: getting served quickly and out of there. Next, look at the alternatives. You could push to the front of the queue (not a wise option) or if you're in a queue of traffic, you could park your car and walk away (not very practical). Perhaps it doesn't really matter if you're delayed for a while, or you could come back another day.

Once you've practiced letting go of some smaller fixed outcomes, you might be able to let go of the larger ones and discover a deeper truth: sometimes when we stop trying to make things happen, we open ourselves up to a whole world of alternative and unanticipated outcomes. (See the exercise "Being *and* doing" in chapter seven and look at "comparative thinking" in chapters six, seven, and eight, which puts every outcome into one of two categories: good or bad.)

Depression = separation from true self

If you don't listen to your feelings, and what they are trying to tell you, you can end up living a life dictated by others (your parents, your boss, or your partner) or buying into the values of others (our materialistic and consumer-orientated society). Personally, I can think of nothing more depressing than believing that you are on the wrong path—especially in your forties and fifties when you are aware that nobody, not even you, is immortal. I know these feelings are challenging and you may be worried about the impact of your discoveries on others. However, finding your true self brings great rewards and does not necessarily mean taking a wrecking ball to your life.

If this is you: focus on chapter five—Turning your life around. By getting to know yourself better, you will have a greater chance of finding what makes life meaningful for you. Jung writes: "Meaninglessness inhibits fullness of life and is therefore equivalent to illness. Meaning makes a great many things endurable—perhaps everything."

WHAT IS THE OPPOSITE OF DEPRESSION?

Sometimes the best way to clarify something is to think about its opposite. While a lot of people imagine the opposite of depression is gaiety or an absence of pain, the true opposite is vitality and experiencing the full kaleidoscope of human emotions. I will explain how to fire up your energy and how that is inextricably linked to being truly aware of your feelings.

EXERCISE RECORD YOUR FEELINGS

When we're asked by friends, colleagues, or family members about our day or our weekend, we tend to think of blocks of time and report back our black and white feelings. We've had a "good" or "bad" day and our weekend was "exhausting" or "relaxing." Once you become more aware of your feelings, the picture is far more complex and even if you're feeling depressed this will not be the only emotion that you have experienced.

The best way to be more mindful of your emotions is to keep a record of your feelings either in a notebook that you carry with you or on your phone.

1. Divide the page into three columns. In the first put the time, in the second record the feeling, and in the third the trigger—this could be an event (getting up for breakfast or arriving home) or a thought ("we haven't had sex for three weeks" or "I hate my job").

2. Make certain you are truly recording a *feeling*. I often find that people put thoughts in this section.

3. I'd like you record at least eight feelings a day. This sounds like a lot but once you start to register them, you'll find you've hundreds each day. For example, just reading this exercise, you could be feeling

exasperated ("He's asking me to do something else" or "He doesn't realize that my life is falling apart and all he's doing is tinkering at the edges") and curious ("I wonder how many feelings I do have") and excitement ("Maybe I'm not aware of my feelings and knowing myself better could help").

4. Don't judge your own feelings, just be curious and name them. (I know this is hard and if you find yourself doing this, write "self-judgmental" and try to be compassionate; it takes time to change.)

5. Update your record in quiet moments during the day.

6. Please keep this record for five days before you review the process. Even if you're generally depressed, I hope you will find that you actually experienced a variety of emotions, however mild (like an inner smile over something amusing on TV or pleasure when a friend calls). But if recording your emotions tips you into a darker place, please stop immediately and consult your doctor.

Important: I'd like you to stop reading the rest of this exercise until you've recorded your feelings for five days so you don't prejudice your findings; just move on to the next section.

1. After five days, look for patterns. Are there feelings that regularly come and go? Why might that be? How do your thoughts affect your feelings? What surprised you?

2. How evenly spread are your feelings? It could be that you don't even register your more pleasant emotions. (I often find that people think "feelings" equals difficult emotions and don't record or really remember their happy times.)

3. Feelings can be grouped into families—for instance, shock (including surprise, confusion, and amazement); anger (including annoyance, resentment, and rage); sadness (including disappointment, hurt, and despair); fear (including worry, anxiety, shame); love (including appreciation, compassion, sexiness); disgust (including aversion, scorn, and revulsion); happiness (including contentment, amusement, and joy) and numbness (including chilled, autopilot, and disconnected).

You might not agree with my groupings and please feel free to compile your own. My aim is to show the possible range of feelings that you might experience. Is there any family of feelings that you haven't recorded?

4. Are your feelings at the mild end? Take the family that you find particularly problematic and draw up your own scale, from mild to strong. For example, with anger, it could be: upset, annoyed, pissed, angry, incensed, furious, ballistic.

5. Keep the diary for another five days and review again. Are you recording a greater range of feelings now? You might discover that you're experiencing two or three emotions at the same time. This is particularly the case with frustration, which normally hides several other feelings. Sadness, for example, can include nostalgia or bitterness or regret or anger.

6. I hope you will discover something incredibly important through this exercise: no feeling lasts forever. On the one hand, it's a shame that we can't be happy all the time. However, it is incredibly comforting: another feeling will be along in a minute (and it might be easier to cope with than the last). Don't believe me, look back over your diary; you have the proof.

7. The other advantage of recording your feelings is that you will be more aware, more grounded, and have more clues for solving the questions of the middle passage.

WHAT HAPPENS IF YOU LISTEN TO YOUR FEELINGS

I have an acquaintance whose wife died of cancer. Six months after the funeral, and as we walked our dogs through the forest, he told me how he was doing.

"When I was a soldier I saw terrible things," he said. "I thought it had made me strong, so I wouldn't be too badly affected, but how wrong I've been. There are days when I literally can't do anything more than let the dog out of the back door."

I had a lot of empathy for this man for I thought I could manage my own grief, because I was a therapist. My goodness, I was naive.

My acquaintance continued: "Just before the funeral, I read this article about 7/11 breathing—how to breathe in to the count of seven and out for the count of eleven—and how it could control your feelings. I was worried about breaking down at the funeral, so I started practicing and got so good at it that I could just say to myself '7/11' and I'd snap out of it. Except nowadays, for no particular reason, I feel defeated and it's stopped working."

"Have you tried accepting your feelings instead?" I said to him.

My simple reply came as a complete revolution to him. From the look on this ex-soldier's face, I might have suggested going into a war zone without a gun.

There are seven advantages to first accepting your feelings and then listening to them:

Reduces the power of the critical voice inside

I know how unpleasant it can feel to grieve. By trying to control his feelings, my dog-walking acquaintance was not only dealing with the pain of loss but a nasty internal voice saying: "Pull yourself together" and "You've cried enough." Adversity is tough enough without adding a layer of self-criticism on top. So be compassionate with yourself, and remember to practice good self-care. There is probably a good reason why life feels hard even if you can't pinpoint why straight away.

Takes the edge off difficult feelings

If you accept your feelings rather than pushing them away, you can begin to truly witness them (and that's the first step to understanding them). The crucial part of witnessing is naming your feelings. Recently I was invited to the wedding of my deceased partner's nephew. Underneath a fresh wave of loss, I named sadness but also pride that I could represent my partner. If I hadn't listened to the pain, I would not have registered the full complexity of my emotions. The sadness included my nostalgic memory of going to this nephew's confirmation together; also, I was pleased to be remembered and invited. So if I'd been asked to score the pain when the invitation arrived, I would have said a seven (out of ten), but when I named my feelings overall, the pain had subsided to a five. I was dealing with old, less raw emotions—but even a reduction from a ten to a nine is a step in the right direction, and reduces the chance of a knee-jerk emotional reaction.

Stops you dividing feelings into good or bad

Our society likes to divide emotions into good (more please) and bad (no thank you). So anger is seen as a bad emotion because it can be ugly and destructive. I would challenge that idea. Anger also provides energy and a sense that something needs to be done. Meanwhile, love is good because it promotes kindness and generosity; but we have all seen people do terrible things in the name of love including accepting abusive behavior. Returning to grief, if I hadn't grieved fully for my first partner I would not have been able to open my heart again. So try not to divide emotions into good or bad but accept them for what they are.

Helps you to come off autopilot

One of the great problems of the modern world is that we're all so busy we don't register what's happening right under our noses. I'm not just talking about stopping to smell the coffee, savor it, and truly taste it—rather than bolting it back for the caffeine kick—although that's important. If you are aware of your feelings, you are less likely to fall into a trap that I call "bottle and blow." This is where you are so used to suppressing your feelings that it happens automatically—without you even registering. The best way to describe this phenomenon is living on autopilot (and as you're beginning to realize, we're not going to live forever so why waste chunks not being truly aware). The other advantage of coming off autopilot is improved communication. There are only so many emotions that can be contained in a bottle before it explodes as ranting and name-calling (at one end of the scale) and snide remarks or general snappiness (at the other).

Promotes inner calm

If you accept your emotions, don't self-judge and become truly aware of them, you have a choice as to how you react. This will help to promote inner calm. Instead of acting out anger, for example, by slamming doors or driving too fast, you could report your feelings: "I am feeling angry." In the same way that naming your feelings to yourself takes the edge off them, saying them out loud increases the effect. It is also provides people around you with important information. Perhaps they thought you were just upset (and need to take your feelings more seriously) or feared that you were vengeful (and therefore can come off high alert). It is much easier to listen to someone who tells you (calmly) that they are angry than if they shout at you or give you the silent treatment. This will encourage your partner, children, work colleagues, or friends to be calmer around you and communicate better too.

Deal with the pinches and avoid the crunches

If your natural response is to minimize, suppress, or intellectualize your feelings, you are unlikely to deal with issues as they happen. So instead of, perhaps, saying, "I don't want to go to your mother's on Sunday," you go along and feel resentful. I call these smaller incidents "pinches" but if you save up enough pinches—and never get a chance to do what you want to do on a Sunday—you end up with a major incident or what I call a "crunch," for example, accusing your partner of being controlling. While it is reasonably straightforward to negotiate over what you're doing this Sunday (for example going to your mother-in-law for only an hour, your partner visiting alone, or your partner choosing the activity this weekend and you choose next time around), when an argument is no longer about a specific incident but has become about the other person's character it is much harder to unpick. Fortunately, there is a solution: listening to your feelings will provide the impetus to speak out in a timely manner, open negotiations, find a compromise, and resolve the pinch—thereby avoiding a future crunch.

Allows you to trust your guts

Instead of listening to the messages you remember from your parents, society, or what is deemed current common sense, you start to develop an inner compass. If something feels painful or difficult, you will register this and work out how to respond. Feelings are clues rather than instructions—and just because something feels pleasurable does not make it morally right. Slowly but surely, you will begin to put together a map of these challenging areas. The more accurate your map, the better your decisions will be. Eventually, you will build up enough positive experiences to trust your own judgment rather than feeling you must canvas others for their views.

EXERCISE | EMOTIONAL RESCUE

It is tough to listen to your feelings especially when they are painful, overwhelming, or promote anxiety. Try this simple counting meditation:

1. Close your eyes, sit upright, and put your hands in your lap. (If it's not possible to close your eyes, focus on a point straight ahead.)

2. Become aware of the air entering your nostrils and exiting them.

3. Take a few deep and slow breathes and anchor your attention to your breathing.

4. When you're ready, take a breath and hold it for a second. Say or think the number ten and slowly exhale.

5. Once again inhale and hold but this time say the number nine and exhale.

6. Repeat the process and count down to zero.

7. If you find yourself distracted, focus back on the sensation of the air passing into and out of your nostrils.

8. Once you've reached zero, take another breath, hold it, and say the number one again.

9. Repeat the process and count back up to ten.

10. At this point, you can either stop and open your eyes or repeat the process.

You will find the counting meditation is very calming: it not only ensures you're taking a good lungful of oxygen but provides a short break from your ruminating mind. You might like to do this simple meditation a couple of times a day.

WHAT HAPPENS IF YOU PAY ATTENTION TO YOUR THOUGHTS

If you did the exercise in chapter one about naming your thought patterns, you will already have started to *pay attention* to your thoughts as opposed to *listening* to them. So what is the difference?

Paying attention means objectively acknowledging your thought processes, rather than getting caught up in individual thoughts. It is a much slower process than listening in which you might skip straight to acting on your thoughts (not always wise in depression) without testing whether they are true or not. The benefits of observing your thoughts and slowing down your reactions will become clearer as I work through the following points:

Become conscious of automatic thinking

If you have been ignoring your feelings, you may be fighting a torrent of thoughts instead—a lot of which will be disturbing and unpleasant. Unfortunately, we tend to avoid paying attention to these thoughts by keeping busy, turning on the TV, or turning up the radio in the car and immersing ourselves in interactive games. (On a personal note, I love to escape into a good novel.) Our thoughts don't actually disappear but run alongside these activities. It's almost like the background noise of traffic, or the hum of the refrigerator—we know they are there but are not fully conscious of them. I call this process automatic thinking and I've spent the last few years gathering the most common messages that are running in the background of the brains of people in their forties and fifties:

- I'm a failure.

- I'm not good enough.

- I'm not going to find love again.

- I can't do anything right.

- I'm not attractive enough.

- What's the matter with me?

- What have I done with my life?

- I'm not getting any younger.

Opportunity to challenge your thoughts

Many of your automatic thoughts will be unappetizing and depressing. Your thought patterns might be judgmental, self-critical, or castastrophizing. If you really pay attention to both the core messages and the destructive thinking patterns, you can begin to challenge them:

Act like a secretary: imagine that you are taking dictation from your boss. Don't question or debate but simply write the monologue down. It will look different in black and white and you will be surprised to discover that there is less to read than you imagined (because it is often the same thoughts going round and round).

Act like a barrister: cross-examine yourself. What is the evidence that your life is a mess? Where are the exaggerations? How much of the evidence is simply hearsay? Are you taking evidence from one part of your life (like your private life) and applying it to another (for example, your career)? What is the case for the defense?

Act like an editor: a good editor will challenge absolute or sloppy language. The aim is to note the times when you do this yourself. Even a small change from "I always lose my temper" to "I sometimes lose my temper" will have an impact on how you view yourself and the world around you. I would also root out the phrases "I should" or "I must." Who says you "should" or "must" do something? Would it be more accurate if you were to say "My mother says I should . . ." rather than "I should?" Or "I believe my job is to solve everything" rather than "I must find a solution?"

Act like a journalist: a good reporter should arrive at an incident with no preconceptions and report accurately and objectively on what he or she sees.

How would the report from the journalist read if you reframed the monologue (from the secretary), using the evidence (extracted by the barrister), and removing the sloppy language (spotted by the editor)?

| EXERCISE | **DISCOVER THE LINK BETWEEN THOUGHTS AND FEELINGS** |

If you've been keeping a record of your feelings, you'll have discovered that feelings are often triggered by thoughts rather than events. To help you discover the link between your thoughts and your feelings, use the following the framework:

A is Adversity

B is for Belief (or thought)

C is for Consequence (or feeling)

Here is an example from one of my clients:

A: Adversity is my partner binging on cocaine.

B: Belief is that it's a reaction to my unreasonable behavior.

C: Consequence is that I feel distraught and angry with myself.

Here is an alternative reading of my client's experience and shows how challenging the thought can impact on the feeling:

A: Partner binges on cocaine

B: My partner is responsible for his own choices

C: I'm still upset but calmer and feeling less responsible.

Why don't you try finding links between your thoughts and feelings during a regularly challenging situation in your life, using the same framework?

A:

B:

C:

Learn that you can't solve the problem of your emotions

There is often a gap between how you *do* feel and how you think you *should* feel. Unfortunately, your mind is always trying to sort out your problems and so will keep asking: "What's wrong with *me?*"

If you believe that you should always be happy (being in a good mood, having pleasant experiences, or avoiding struggle and pain), you will try to solve any unhappiness. For example, you could wake up at the weekend feeling sad or tired. If you haven't yet learned to accept your feelings, you are likely to want to solve the problem of feeling sad or tired. You will start going through everything that's wrong with your life—wondering if that's the source of feeling sad—and before long fall into ruminating, automatic thinking, and other destructive habits.

Remember, feelings aren't problems in themselves. Once you've taken this idea on board, you could accept that you've woken up feeling sad and just get on with your day, because we have lots of feelings every day and a different feeling will shortly come along. This will help you to avoid allowing a momentary low pull you into a downward cycle that ruins your whole day.

See thoughts for what they are

We all have a narrative for our lives based on past events but mainly constructed by our interpretations of those events which, in turn, are fed through our day-to-day thoughts. This narrative—even if it is wrong or full of partial truths—impacts on our behavior today and provides a reference point for the future. In mindfulness—a treatment rooted in Buddhist philosophy that is used for both depression and managing anxiety—there is a useful image: thoughts are not carved in stone but rather written on water. I love this idea because it provides a very fluid narrative for our thoughts rather than a fixed one.

Hopefully, you are beginning to see thoughts as simply thoughts —rather than facts. A thought arises, lingers in our consciousness for a short period of time, and then fades. In effect, thoughts are mental events. You don't have to develop the thought and start to ruminate on it. I know this is a hard concept to digest but the next exercise will help.

EXERCISE SOUND AND THOUGHT MEDITATION

This exercise will deepen your understanding of how your thoughts work and how you can stop random thoughts triggering a bout of depression. At first it will seem strange to couple sounds with thoughts, but please be patient with me and everything will be revealed. This exercise will take about ten minutes.

1. *Prepare.* Sit still with your feet on the floor and your hands in your lap or resting on your thighs. Close your eyes.

2. *Focus on your breath.* Become aware of the air going in and out of your nostrils.

3. *Gradually become aware of the sounds around you.* Don't search for them, just be aware as they rise and disappear. Some of them will be nearby and others far away. Notice how one noise will crowd out another.

4. *Find the music in the sounds.* Instead of labeling sounds —perhaps a police siren going past—be aware of the pitch, tone, and tempo. In this way, you stay with the raw sounds and avoid getting caught up in the meanings and stories that we attach to the sounds. (For example, wondering where the police car is going and what the officers might find on arrival.)

5. *Use your breath as an anchor.* If you find your mind wandering or getting caught up with individual sounds, return to your breath, and focus on the air you inhale and exhale.

6. *Stay with the sounds.* It will take about ten minutes to relax and meditate on the sounds.

7. *Gradually become aware of your thoughts.* Like sounds, thoughts rise, linger, and pass away. During the meditation you will have dozens, maybe hundreds, of different thoughts—that's fine.

8. *Visualize your thoughts.* It could be pictures on a screen or clouds passing overhead or some other image that works for you. You don't have to get involved with the thoughts—like the sounds—and make a whole story out of them.

9. *Let the thought pass by.* Like a cloud, another one will come along in a second. You don't have to develop the thought—just label it—and let it pass. (For example, if you are having trouble sleeping, you could picture yourself lying awake in bed and then let it go, rather than developing a whole movie where you are snappy at breakfast and underperforming at work because you're overtired. If you prefer the cloud image, label one thought as "anxiety" or "sleep problems" and let it float on past.)

10. *Note any strong feelings.* If a thought comes with a charge—whether pleasant or unpleasant—simply register it and let it pass as you did with the sounds.

11. *Your breath is still your anchor.* If your thoughts gets scattered or you find yourself getting drawn in, return your attention to your breath. Make certain that you are taking deep slow breaths and spending longer breathing out than in.

This exercise will help you to distance yourself from your thoughts. You will notice how easy it is for some random thought to become a developing thought and get caught in a loop of destructive thinking (with the impact lingering long after the original trigger has passed). Once you become more aware of this train of associations, you can step back onto the platform before the train has left the station!

PULLING IT ALL TOGETHER

Once you become aware of just how many feelings and thoughts you have every day, it is easy to feel overwhelmed. To help you cope, I suggest imagining that you are sitting by a river of feelings and above are clouds passing by carrying particular thoughts. You don't have to worry about the water flowing or the wind blowing the clouds; just take a few deep breaths. If something unpleasant comes up, you're not in the water management business (so you don't need to pump away the feeling), neither do you need to reach up and pull down the cloud (in order to unpack the thought). Equally, if something good flows or floats past, you don't have to dam the river of feelings or lasso the cloud to hold on to it. Your job is to just accept the feelings and observe the thoughts. If that's hard, tell yourself: another feeling or thought will be along in a moment. They might be easier or harder, but remember the essential fact of life: change is the only certainty in life, and therefore nothing lasts forever.

At this point, you may be thinking that my approach might sound calming but your life doesn't make sense any more. Something needs to change and soon! Don't worry, I'm only asking you to be aware of your feelings and thought patterns (in the moment) rather than to accept a bad situation (in the medium or long-term).

If you notice the same feelings coming down the river or the same thoughts floating past in the sky time and time again, that's a really strong message and some action will need to be taken. Let me give you an example.

When Derek, fifty-three, became truly mindful of his feelings and thoughts, he was amazed to realize how much of his life had been governed by fear.

"I've always known that I don't like confrontation and will agree with what other people want in order to avoid a scene," he explained to me, "but not how strong my fear of confrontation had been. If I felt overwhelmed, the shutters would come down and I'd be there but not there."

When he started to really pay attention to this reaction, Derek realized why even mild frustration from his partner would trigger a strong reaction in him.

"If I upset my mother, she would tell me, 'Wait till your father gets home' and he had a terrible temper and would take me into the living room, close the door, and beat me."

I asked what message Derek had taken from his childhood experiences and how that impacted on his day-to-day thoughts.

"That I have to be good to be loved and if I'm not good I'm going to be punished," he concluded.

Once he had paid attention to these thoughts, rather than running them in the background as part of his automatic thinking, Derek could begin to challenge them.

"I spoke to my brother and sister who are much older than me and found the same thing had happened to them. They too had been beaten and felt betrayed by our mother. But they'd had each other to comfort them, while I was alone."

"How has that affected your thoughts?" I asked.

"I don't feel so much that I was a bad or unreasonable child, because it happened to my siblings too. I'm kinder to myself and don't feel so self-critical for messing up when I was small or closing down as an adult."

I hope I've explained how suppressing difficult feelings and having a critical internal voice has a strong link to depression. The more I've worked with people in their forties and fifties, the more I believe that being middle-aged—and facing life's challenges without the comforting embrace of youthful wishful thinking—is more likely to trigger situational depression. It is normal and necessary to retreat into yourself and take stock, but if you don't listen to the wisdom of depression or if you have unresolved issues from childhood, it is not difficult to slip further into clinical depression.

If you've recognized that you're clinically depressed, you need to consult your doctor. If your main problem is a critical inner voice, CBT might be recommended. If you are dealing with more complex issues, you could need therapy that goes deeper. Your doctor may discuss whether medication could be helpful too. I would also recommend my book *Wake Up and Change Your Life: How to survive a crisis and be stronger, wiser, and happier,* and if you'd like to know more about mindfulness, look at the further reading list at the back of this book.

SUMMING UP

➤ Your emotions are not the enemy but an opportunity to be aware of what's happening in your life, and to assess the impact.

➤ There can be wisdom and renewal from depression as long as you take the prompts to be quiet, look inward, and rest. If you repeatedly ignore the invitations to learn, you risk turning feeling down or being depressed into clinical depression.

➤ Learning to accept your feelings and challenge your thoughts is a big step forward in tackling depression.

CHAPTER FOUR

Affairs, the great other, and the danger of shortcuts

Moving from the first to the second half of life can be difficult because it involves a fundamental shift in how you look at both yourself and the world around you. From my therapist point of view, it means a lot of learning and growth. From your viewpoint, it's a lot of pain, heartache, and disruption—so I'm not surprised that you're kicking against the idea or want to find a shortcut. So what is it about the middle passage that is disruptive and why it is so necessary?

I describe the shift as going from being focused on the outer world (possessions, status, and success) to your inner world (who you really are). One of the best ways to explain this is going from thinking about your CV to thinking about your eulogy. When I explained this idea to one of my clients, Kevin, forty-eight, a partner in a big city law firm who was trying to rebuild his marriage after an affair, he immediately got the idea.

"One of the senior partners died, the other week, of a heart attack," he said. "He was a great lawyer, he'd really get his teeth stuck into a case, not let go and he billed a lot of hours. But he wasn't a particularly nice person and nobody at the firm *really* liked him. So at his funeral, everything was a bit flat, and the eulogy was all about his achievements rather than him as a person. I want something more in my eulogy than 'He won a lot of cases.'"

That's one of the great advantages of being forty- or fifty-something—Kevin was beginning to see the bigger picture. If he had been in his twenties and thirties, he would have been too busy climbing the ladder and building a secure place in the outer world to truly understand how empty the eulogy had been. Even the idea of someone standing by his coffin to sum up his life would have been simply preposterous. But Kevin had already begun to entertain that possibility: "I want my children to think I was a good man and a good father, not a cheat and a liar."

Another way at looking at this change is that we go from worrying about the roles we play, the masks we choose to wear and living up to others' expectations to finding our true self. If we're lucky this can involve moving from having a job to having a vocation. (More about this in the next chapter).

Many people think this shift from the first (outer) to second (inner) world is a new phenomenon because we're all living longer. However, the French essayist and philosopher Michel de Montaigne (1533–1592) went through just such a transformation. He lived the sixteenth-century version of being a success: he was a town councilor, a member of the local parliament, and was woken sweetly every morning with music played by hired musicians. At thirty-eight, he gave up all these outward trappings, retired to his library, and famously wrote: "Every man rushes elsewhere into the future, because no man has arrived at himself."

THE LURE OF THE SHORTCUT

We think the push for glory in the external world will bring us tranquillity in the internal one, because it may have brought us a kind of contentment in the first half of our life. By our forties and fifties, we're beginning to sense that there is something more: a better-balanced, more expansive version of ourselves—what I call our true self. The power of magical, heroic, and wishful thinking is waning and we are getting ready to face the full complexity—and I would say glory—of being alive.

Unfortunately, it is hard to listen to the call from our true self and many people fall into depression or are gripped by anxiety. If you're depressed it is easy to convince yourself that you need a quick solution and that if something is hard then it is fundamentally wrong.

Sarah, forty, had temporarily separated from her husband, Daniel, forty-five, because she found him controlling and their relationship lacked passion. They had a 4-year-old child together. She had agreed to come to couple counseling and Daniel hoped I would help her fall back in love with him. Sarah was open to this idea but was more focused on learning to communicate properly with Daniel and being better co-parents. Unpacking the baggage from the past and beginning to confront, rather than avoid, day-to-day issues had rebuilt their relationship to the point that they started to have sex again. Unfortunately, Sarah was returning to Canada (her home country) for an extended vacation, so it was four months until I next saw them.

During this period, Daniel went to Canada to visit his wife. He recognized almost straight away that it had been a mistake because Sarah wanted time on her own. Rather than using the communication skills I'd taught them, they dropped back into their old roles: he pussyfooted around her (tried to keep the peace) and she seethed inside (but was outwardly pleasant). They had not talked about any of this until they were in their car on the way to my office.

"We find communication fundamentally hard," Sarah sighed deeply. "It's what I keep saying: 'If it's this tough then it can't be right.' We should both find ourselves a different relationship where we don't have to struggle and it's all straightforward. Everything between us needs so much work."

"The last time I saw you, you'd just started to have sex and the experience was good." I wanted to query the distance that had grown between this session and the last one.

"That's another example; it didn't feel weird to have sex or to kiss Daniel—which had been my fear—but the passion didn't flow freely." Although I had sympathy for Sarah's frustration, I don't believe that a good relationship is an easy one because I have an innate suspicion of easy solutions. It is often magical, heroic, or wishful thinking or another kind of shortcut—the great other—that makes it harder to find our true self.

THE GREAT OTHER

Of all the myths in the world, the most powerful one must be what I call the great other. One day, someone will come along and recognize our true worth, rescue us from this vale of tears, and put us up where we belong. Perhaps the best loved version of this myth is the fairy-tale Cinderella. Experts on story and myths, like Joseph Campbell, believe that there are only seven basic plots in the whole world, and this one is the most popular. The great other provides a shortcut (or if I'm being more poetic "rescues" or even "saves" us) and comes in several forms—not just a handsome prince or the beautiful princess. Whatever the incarnation, the great other will:

1. Meet your needs.

2. Take care of you.

3. Always be there for you.

4. Validate you (because you must be worthy if someone special believes in you).

And who wouldn't want a bit of that! The great other is such a powerful myth and when we're provisional adults trying to get ourselves established in the world, the pull is particularly strong. So let's look at five areas where the great other is most likely to operate:

Career

I have been on the board of a charity that helps new and emerging writers. Needless to say, I've met a lot of writers at every stage of their career. So what do you think writers talk about? I'm afraid it isn't the glory of words or the complexity of plot but how much they dislike their agents! As you can imagine, it is a bit frightening for new writers because they are desperate to find themselves an agent but they comfort themselves by thinking "I will find a good one." (I know because that's what I used to think.) Recently, I chaired a discussion about how to find an agent and the agents on the panel started by describing their role, which included: developing writers' careers, making connections, ensuring that publishers sell and market their writers' books correctly, and defending their copyrights. In other words, agents will meet your needs and take care of you and as their contract involves taking a percentage on the books they sell for the rest of your life—plus seventy years (the length of copyright)—they will always be there for you. Their validation will lift you out of the pile of unsolicited manuscripts that arrive at publishers' offices every day. All the potential writers in the audience were salivating.

Unfortunately, in order to make a living, agents need to represent a lot of writers so can't offer as personal a service as they would like. Publishers release a lot of books—to their best of their ability—so they can only allocate a small amount of their resources to each title (and even the best and most powerful agent in the world can't change this simple truth). Ultimately, every writer is responsible for his or her own career development. So in the question and answer session, I suggested the writers could self-publish, which would allow them to keep creative control and receive a larger slice of the cover price of their books. There was barely a flicker of interest in the idea because who wants to be bothered with finding an editor, a proofreader, a designer, and learning about distribution channels when the promise of the great other is so seductive?

You will have come across potential great others in your workplace too. It might be a senior member of staff who promises to mentor you through the ranks or a colleague who is starting up a business that will allow you to achieve all of your ambitions.

Organizations

I've mentioned that my first career was in local radio. My employers were very paternalistic. It was a new company and they started a share scheme for employees so we could all benefit from its success. We were given station T-shirts and sweatshirts to wear every day. I was a member of the on-air talent team and the company found us all free sponsored cars from local garages and allowed us to accept exotic vacations in return for broadcasting reports about the vacation locations. All the staff received a Christmas bonus, and one year a free turkey too. In return, I often worked seven days a week and spent a lot of my free time opening fêtes, judging beautiful baby competitions, and generally promoting the radio station. The company met my needs and took care of me.

One evening, I was in the managing director's office listening to him chat with his number two (my line manager). "We have a really good team," said the MD, "and we're all very pally, but someday we're going to have to let some of them go." In effect, he was warning his number two not to get too close to his staff.

I was pleased to learn this valuable truth at a relatively young age that organizations might provide status, but they could also take it away. Despite the job satisfaction, I only stayed with the company for three years.

You will have come across a lot of organizations with pretensions to be the great other. It could be an employer, a political party, a religious, or social group. Alternatively, it could be something more amorphous like a country or even an idea (like the United Nations).

Parenting

A powerful incarnation of the great other is our children. I am sure you know someone who hopes their child will fulfill all their dreams. The classic example is the stage-door mother and the soccer-coach father. In most cases the relationship is more subtle, but there is still an element of living through the kids.

Although it is our job to take care of our children and fulfill their needs, these roles can easily get turned around. Our joy that our children are doing well at school can become more about our need to be reassured that we're doing a good job as a parent; our worry about them going off to "big" school is less about what might happen to them there and more about us no longer being the center of their lives. I have had many clients who as children had to comfort their own mother or father through a divorce and support them through the next crisis. They had always been there for their parent and met their needs. In the process, the needs of my clients—often still single in their thirties and forties—were still coming second.

Relationships

It is extremely difficult to admit just how much we expect of our partners and so probably a little embarrassing to see our expectations laid out on the page. But if you're being honest, how many of these statements ring true?

"I am counting on you to make my life meaningful."

"I am counting on you to always be there for me."

"You will read my mind and anticipate my deepest needs."

"You will bind my wounds, complete me, and make me whole again."

"You will heal my stricken soul."

"Your love will lift me up and thereby validate my worth in the world."

OK, you might give a wry smile because the day-to-day reality of living together is very different: "Sure you're always there for me, so why do you insist on going outside for a late-night cigarette rather than coming up to bed?" It also begs the question: can you make someone else's life meaningful? After all, it's hard enough finding your own meaning in life and if, by some miracle, you did have a formula for your beloved, you'd probably be accused of being controlling.

The promise of love in most pop songs—"You light up my life," "Wind beneath my wings," "With you I'm born again," "My world is empty without you"—points to our fundamental belief in the great other. In the first flush of love we believe that we have found our great other—otherwise who would link their future with a relative stranger's?

Guru

After writing the proposal for my book *I Love You But I'm Not in Love With You* ten years ago, I was in the fortunate position that five or six companies wanted to publish it. My agent took me to meet the competing teams of editors and their marketing departments. As we were walking to the first meeting, my agent worried about something I'd written and whether his own relationship might be in danger. I sought to reassure him.

"Don't worry, I don't have all the answers," I added.

He turned to me immediately. "Whatever you do, don't say anything like that in our meeting," he said. "They want to believe that you know *everything* about relationships."

In other words, they were looking for the great other, too. Interestingly enough some of the publishers I met subsequently contacted me with their relationship problems. I've had people fly from South America to meet me for a series of counseling appointments. I try and explain that sitting in my office does not magic away their problems and they still have to face their own demons and learn the appropriate skills themselves (but I wonder if the message is always heard).

The term guru comes from Sanskrit and is best translated as "spiritual leader." Since our Western society's crisis in faith (best illustrated by the famous quote from the nineteenth-century German philosopher Friedrich Nietzsche, "God is dead"), lots of self-proclaimed experts and teachers have presented themselves as the great other, or perhaps have had the role thrust on them by people desperate to believe in something.

WHY ARE THERE SO MANY MIDLIFE AFFAIRS?

In the first half of our lives, we invested in roles to make our lives meaningful—career, maybe marriage, parenting, etc. With the confidence of youth, backed up with heroic thinking, we were determined not to make the same mistakes as our parents. Magical thinking made us invest in the idea that someone would come along and take away all our doubts and fears. We still had an unspoken contract with the universe: if I have a good heart and good intentions, everything will turn out fine (wishful thinking).

By the middle passage—usually the section between the first and second half of your life—you have enough experience of the world to question these simplistic beliefs. You might have chanced upon a great other for your career but he or she had his or her own agenda or got distracted in some other project or left the company. You might have invested heavily in an organization but not had your needs met or discovered a gap between their expressed values and what happens in practice. Your children may have reached the sullen adolescent stage and are desperately resisting your demands. They are also on a journey to becoming who they are—rather than who you would like them to be (or need them to be). Hopefully, you are beginning to see the truth that parenting is about nurturing (the easier half) *and* empowering (the harder part because it means bringing up your children to leave you).

If you expected your partner to complete you, to be your soul mate (a phrase that makes me profoundly uncomfortable because a soul mate can easily be perceived as a great other) and always be there for you, my guess is that he or she has often let you down. He or she is made of flesh and blood, rather than a knight in shining armor, a personal therapist, and an ever-willing sex toy. No wonder many people complain to their beloved: "You're not the person I married"—or to be accurate: "You're not the fantasy version of you that I thought I married, but a stranger who I only know a little better now."

At this point, I hope you are beginning to question whether the great other really exists ... or maybe not. You could be rebelling against the idea. "Nobody is going to 'save' me! Help!" At this point, it might seem that I've turned from a therapist and author into a spoil sport who has let slip that there is no Santa Claus, Tooth Fairy, or Easter Bunny. But don't worry, the situation is not as bleak as it seems at first sight. I have lots of adult coping strategies to teach and you are not completely alone. (More on this later in the chapter.)

If your life does not make sense any more, you are depressed and lacking in energy and your partner is often angry or disappointed, it seems easier to go down a different path. Instead of questioning whether the great other exists (and rolling up your sleeves, dealing with the questions of the middle passage, and the problems in your marriage), you tell yourself: "I haven't met him or her yet." In effect, you made a mistake when you got married and need to tell your partner "I never loved you" or "We're different people" and start looking around for someone else who will complete you and make life meaningful again. More likely, if you are not someone given to introspection, all these thoughts were grinding away in your unconscious, and someone has popped up—at work, at play, or over the Internet—who made your heart beat faster. There was chemistry. You shared all the same interests and he or she thought you were wonderful. Unlike conversations with your partner—which have been encrusted with no-go areas, habit, and the business of day-to-day life—you can *really* talk to this new love interest.

Your conclusion, naturally enough, is that the great other *does* exist and you've just met him or her! And now you're prepared to betray your partner and family because "this thing is bigger than both of us." You're going to hate me for saying this, but you have just taken a shortcut.

THE DOWNSIDE OF THE AFFAIR PARTNER AS THE GREAT OTHER

For the first time in years, you feel alive again. You have the energy of someone ten or maybe twenty years younger. You feel properly understood, the sex is incredible, and there is a real connection. What could possibly go wrong?

Affairs are built on fantasy

I know I am stating the obvious but affairs happen in secret and are not tested in the real world. You cannot invite your lover to meet your friends or family and even if he or she is single, your lover will still be concerned about his or her friends' reactions (at least in the formative early stages of the relationship). So there is no need to listen to the inner voices of caution that say: "She's half your age" or "But he only talks about himself." In this bubble world, *projection* (where we see what we want to see in someone and then act as if our beliefs were true) is even stronger. If you project onto someone that he or she is fascinating, you'll look for evidence that backs this up and ignore the ten shelves of *Star Trek* boxsets in their living room (or whatever interest usually leaves you cold).

Unlike regular relationships that are built on extended time together, affairs are built on snatched moments. Instead of slowly increasing levels of intimacy and self-exposure—meeting his difficult mother or her son from her first marriage—the affair deepens by making increasingly grand statements about your feelings ("I have never felt like this before" or "You are my one and only true love") and making extravagant plans for the future. In this vacuum, projection—which is present whenever we meet new people—is going to be much stronger than reality.

I had one client, David, forty-eight, who even visited potential schools with his mistress for the children (from their respective marriages) to attend after they ran away together. His wife, Diana, had found out about the affair and her husband's many deceptions and found it impossible to believe him when he told her the affair had meant nothing.

"How would our children have felt about being uprooted to another town and going to the same school as her children?" she said. "It makes no sense on any level."

David and his mistress had built fantasy on top of fantasy and, in his words, "Even when I was walking around the schools, I never thought it would really happen, but it seemed like a good idea at the time."

Once the fantasy bubble had broken, David found it impossible to recognize the person that he'd been during the affair.

Veronica had two young children but after ten years of marriage, she felt her husband was pulling away and she was afraid her marriage was over.

"I am very insecure and began to feel angry and needed to do something to avoid the humiliation and sadness of divorce."

She saw the opportunity to have an affair with one of her husband's friends but they were discovered and Veronica's husband did divorce her.

"I have a relationship of sorts with this man but for the last six months I've been waiting for him to divorce too and getting fed up with him using every excuse in the books as to why he can't.

"Worse still, I can't even be sure I love this man as he was just there at a time in my life when I had nothing to help me. Our sex life is beyond boring and all our friends have boycotted us and so we seldom go out together."

Limerence does not last forever

Scientists have scanned the brains of people in the early stages of love and identified the chemicals—dopamine, phenylethylamine, and oxytocin—that promote the euphoric walking-on-air feeling when we only have eyes for our beloved, and even if someone with movie-star looks sat down beside us we would not be distracted by them. Psychologists call this phenomena limerence (which I've written about in *I Love You But I'm Not in Love With You*). Under its influence, even if we can see our beloved's potential flaws, they become assets, not cons. For example, Brian, forty-four, fell for Charlotte, forty, a few weeks after his marriage imploded:

"She was very honest with me about her past and how she had just finished a twelve-step program to deal with her cocaine use. I admired her strength of character. We've both had a difficult life and can support each other," he said.

Brian wasn't thinking: "What if she has a relapse?" In his mind, her past was an asset: "we've both been through difficult times and can support each other."

If a friend who understood the complexity of addiction and the problems of relapse had pointed out the potential dangers, Brian would have brushed away these concerns—partly because of wishful thinking, but mainly because he believed their love would be strong enough to ford streams and climb mountains. It is limerence that inspires the writers of popular songs and it is the foundation for many of the myths of love. Meanwhile, his girlfriend was probably ignoring the advice given by many clinics not to form a committed relationship in the first months after rehab, because of the danger of using the high of limerence to replace the high from drugs (and thereby cross-addicting).

What none of us want to hear is *limerence does not last forever.* The feel-good chemicals stay at their peak for somewhere between six and eighteen months, and slowly subside after that until by three years the effect is mainly over.

You've turned your partner into the great enemy

When your marriage was going well, you put any problems down to something external and fleeting. For example, your partner's moodiness on a vacation was down to the bad weather (and being stuck inside a cottage while the rain lashed against the window) or stress from work (following a long and intensive project). With this mindset, any unpleasantness is quickly put to one side and forgotten. But when your marriage is in serious trouble, you stop blaming the circumstances and focus on something fixed: your partner's character. So his or her moodiness is not a passing issue but an illustration of why you no longer love him or her. The problem is not the weather but due to the fact that you are completely different (for example, you look on the bright side but he or she is a pessimist). With this mindset, every example of unpleasantness is noted and added to the reasons why your marriage is fundamentally flawed (and maybe why you deserve or need your affair partner).

In effect, you have entered the drama triangle where you are the victim, your affair partner is the rescuer (the great other), and your partner is the persecutor (the great enemy) who is standing in the way of your happiness.

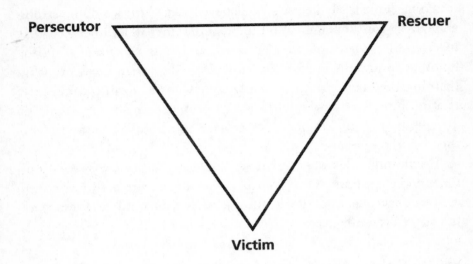

The nature of the drama triangle is that nothing is fixed. In your partner's eyes, he or she is the victim (of your affair) and the other man or woman is the persecutor, and your partner is looking to you to become the rescuer (and end the affair). When you find this difficult (or impossible), you become the persecutor. A triangle is one of the strongest shapes and hardest to break. Sometimes a triangle of relationships can continue for years and can cause immense damage to all three parties.

Your affair partner is not neutral

After my partner died, to my eternal shame I became the third part of an affair triangle. I deeply regret the hurt I caused. As I have spent much of this book chronicling other people's mistakes, it seems only fair that I share mine too.

During the affair, which lasted for about six months, I spent many hours listening to my lover's problems and I was certainly not neutral. I would encourage any doubts about my lover's relationship. I feel ashamed to confess it but I saw my lover as the victim, I was going to be the rescuer and you can guess who I thought was the persecutor.

Perhaps you can really talk to your affair partner and he or she may have endless time to listen. (I would drop everything, including work deadlines, to answer the phone.) Nevertheless, he or she is holding up a distorting mirror and is likely to encourage anything that runs down your partner and paints him or her as the great enemy.

Your affair partner thinks you are the great other too

It was only eighteen months after my partner died that the affair started. At the time, I thought I'd completely recovered and I was ready to make a new long-term relationship. (I feel nothing but pity for my naive 38-year-old self—19 years later I'm still finding new layers of loss.) The reality, back then, was that I hadn't even been through the cupboards deciding what had sentimental value, what to pass on, and what to throw away. I was a mess. I needed saving myself.

When you're in a difficult place, you can be so focused on your need for someone with broad shoulders to make everything right that you can forget that your great other is human too. They have a matching set of problems and a whole lot of unspoken expectations to put on your already overburdened shoulders. Think of the image of the drowning man: the danger is that if you swim out and try to save him, in his panic he'll pull you under. With affairs there are two people in trouble flailing about in deep water; double the danger and double the chance of drowning.

The W-shaped life

One of the worst parts of my recovery from bereavement was when my affair collapsed. (It became clear that our relationship was going nowhere and I ended it.) Not only was I still struggling with mourning for my partner who had died, but also for the future that I'd imagined with this new lover. In addition, I still had to face the existential questions about the meaning of life—one which had been made more acute for me, watching my partner struggle for breath, being that none of us are immortal. Rather than saving me, my great other had thrown me (or rather I'd thrown myself) back into the second trough of the W. I still had to do the work of the middle passage.

EXERCISE PROGRESSIVE RELAXATION

You may be under a lot of stress at the moment—especially if you are torn between your lover and your wife or husband. My guess is you're not sleeping well, so I have an exercise to aid relaxation. It can be done in the early hours when your brain is racing (to help you go back to sleep) or when you're feeling particularly stressed during the day.

Focus on your breathing

Become aware of the sensation of the air coming into your nostrils as you breathe in and of it going out as you exhale. Take a few slow deep breathes and if you find your mind wandering, return to the sensation of the air coming in and going. Remember your breath is an anchor, always there when you need to ground yourself.

Clench your muscles

Starting with your feet, clench your toes and then point them. Concentrate on the sensation for a moment and make a mental note of how it feels, and then relax ... Let your muscles go limp and the tension drain away. Repeat with the muscles in your legs, buttocks, and lower back. Travel up the body and clench each group in turn. Note the tension and let it go. Next, focus on the stomach muscles and shoulders, clench them too and let the stretch go down your arms and clench your fingers as well. Hold the tension for a couple of deep breaths and let it go again. Finally, scrunch up your face, eyelids, lips, and cheeks. Wrinkle your forehead too. Note the tension, relax, and let it go.

Drain the stress

Take a couple more slow and deep breaths and imagine all of the stress draining out of your biceps, then triceps, and then fingers. Next, imagine the stress pouring out of your toes and finally picture the tension going from your whole body as you breathe out.

Do a body scan

Let your attention wander across your body. Do you feel completely relaxed? Do you need to clench, release, and drain the stress again? That's OK, repeat the process as often as you need. Are there places that still feel particularly tense? Focus on clenching and releasing these muscles until you feel more relaxed. If, at any time, you find your mind wandering or filled with negative thoughts (for example, "I'm hopeless at this exercise") please focus on your breathing and gently nudge the thought away.

MY AFFAIR PARTNER IS THE REAL THING

Whenever I explain the U-shaped life, my clients find the concept really useful … until I reach the great other. At this point, the atmosphere changes and they say: "Yes, but …" So I won't be surprised if you're angry with me. Obviously, I don't know you, your lover, or the very real problems with your partner. Before you give up reading in disgust, let me share some experiences from my casebook. I have some key questions to help you decide the best course of action for you.

My lover is a better fit

The argument goes something like this: "I've changed and I'm a different person from the one who met my partner all those years ago. Unfortunately my partner hasn't grown like I have and we no longer fit together. I've met someone else with whom I do share all these common interests, and who wants the same things as me. Surely it would be in everybody's interests if my partner and I split up. I could then pursue this new relationship and my partner could find someone to whom he or she would be more suited."

Martha, forty-one, came to counseling because her marriage had hit a roadblock and she didn't want to put her son through her own experience. Martha's parents had split up when she was a teenager and she had ended up mothering her mother, father, and subsequently her husband:

"I know my parents were not particularly happy together but they were muddling through. If, after the divorce, they'd found something better perhaps I might have understood, but even after all these years neither of them have found lasting relationships and neither is particularly happy."

Meanwhile, the impact on teenage Martha and her younger sister was huge.

"My mother disappeared with another man and Dad went to pieces. Although I was barely fourteen, I was doing all the shopping and cooking for him and my little sister. He started spending time with the woman across the road whose husband was away in the navy. Dad has always claimed it was innocent, I don't know, but someone told the sailor something else. When he came back from sea, he hammered on our door. I guessed what was about to happen but my sister ran to the door. This demented man came bursting in—yelling and swearing—I tried to stand in his way and protect my father. The sailor shoved past me and I was thrown against a coffee table which broke and I had bruises and a cut. He knocked my father to the ground and started kicking him in the stomach. The police had to be called. It was a nightmare."

Once her mother had found somewhere permanent—with her new boyfriend—Martha and her sister went to live with them.

"It wasn't long before Mom realized her boyfriend was just like Dad: a dreamer. If I'm being honest, he was a total waste of space, especially when he'd been drinking. Eventually, Mom threw him out but guess who supported her, kept her strong when she wavered, and mopped up her tears?"

Key questions: So when limerence has worn off, and you've recognized that some of the attributes that you have projected onto your lover may be wishful thinking and normal life has been resumed, ask yourself: How much better will the fit be now? Will it be worth the sacrifices that I'll have to make and I'll be asking from my family, too?

I know my own feelings

I am torn in two over this argument because I fervently believe that you know what's best for you. Still, I wonder how practiced you are at listening to your emotions and understanding the different layers of feelings. Let me explain by returning to Peter, whom had prioritized what other people wanted for most of his life. He had joined a profession which his father and society in general approved of. When he stepped off the career treadmill for a short while after he qualified, he met his future wife on a journey around the world and although he'd enjoyed their time together, he would have preferred to continue on alone. When she begged him to reconsider, he changed his mind and let her accompany him, which set up the pattern for their future. In other words, he considered her feelings more important than his. The only way to continue in this vein was for Peter to rationalize (it's what the family needs) and downgrade (not listen) his feelings. He had operated almost constantly in this way, from the head, until he fell in love with a work colleague.

"It was like a light went on and suddenly the world was multicolored. The joy when she phoned and we could be together; the excitement of running away from a boring work function and hailing a taxi back to our hotel; the ache when we had to part," Peter told me.

"So after years of ignoring your feelings, you're operating completely from the heart," I replied.

"My new motto is: 'If it feels good, do it,'" he said.

"I've another motto," I said. "'If it feels this right then it can't be wrong.'"

Peter nodded eagerly.

"Except, there's another set of feelings too," I prompted.

"You're right," he said slowly. "I feel guilty when I speak to my children and explain that I can't be home for the weekend. Sometimes I feel doubt that I'm doing the right thing and burst into tears with my wife and beg for a second chance."

"So how do you cope?" I asked him.

"I just have to be strong and fixed on the future," he said.

In other words, from now on Peter was going to have to listen to some of his feelings and ignore the others.

Key questions: In my experience, we need to listen to both our heart *and* our head to make a wise decision (and one that sticks). So first: How good are you at listening to *all* your feelings? Are you more prepared to follow the ones that you consider easier and do you ever shut off the less comfortable feelings? What impact will that have on making a wise decision? Finally, what experiences have you had of making decisions from both the heart and the head?

Love will find a way

I am conflicted about this idea. On one hand, we use myths about love to shut down our rational brain and glide past the problems that are obvious to our friends and family. On the other, I am constantly reminded by the actions of my clients of the power of love and how it helps them to find levels of forgiveness that are truly moving. Love can also help us step into someone else's shoes and be truly empathetic. However, in most second long-term relationships, there are also step-parenting problems to overcome. It can be done but it's asking a lot for love to put everything right (and is best entered into with your eyes fully open).

Philip, forty-eight, had three children from his marriage, and his new partner—falling for her had prompted them both to end their marriages—had two of her own. On the weekends when they had all five, they were dealing with the tastes, interests, and issues of children from seven to seventeen.

"It is almost impossible to find something that works for everybody. So it means leaving my 17-year-old out of things, which she doesn't mind too much because she's keen to be with her friends. But I feel guilty that I'm missing out on time with her," explained Philip.

"His second daughter is a daddy's girl and I'm sorry Philip, but she can be a right madam," cut in his new partner Celeste, thirty-nine.

"Needless to say, there isn't a weekend when there are not tears," Philip said, trying to sooth over the troubled waters.

"Once in a while, we will have a weekend when Philip's kids are with his wife and mine are scheduled to be with their father but my youngest can be clingy and, I'm sorry, I don't want to carry her down from her bedroom—kicking and screaming—and force her into his car."

"I was only saying that giving in to her doesn't make it better."

The tension in the room between them was going through the roof. Both partners felt immense guilt and were trying to compensate by being the best possible parents. With so little wriggle room and so many obstacles, it was hard for love to find a way.

"Sometimes I think you put me last—after everybody else," Philip complained.

"How can you say that, after everything I gave up to be with you?" Celeste snapped back.

Key questions: Think about the impact of a split on each of your children in turn: what problems do you foresee? How will you balance being a great parent with being a great partner? How good will you be at dealing with the inevitable conflicts?

OK. You're probably right ... but what if you're wrong?

By this point, I hope you are mellowing toward me. You realize that I am stressing caution because I think it's in your best interests. And yet, what if you let your lover walk away, your marriage proves to be beyond repair, and you lose everything? As the argument goes, 'It's a risk going off with my lover but it's one that I've simply got to take, otherwise I'd be kicking myself for the rest of my life.'

My concern with relationships that start as affairs is this: Your beloved believes in shortcuts (and so do you). So what happens when life throws up yet another obstacle?

One of the advantages of being a therapist is that I've seen thousands of cases and received countless emails where people have shared their stories (from further down the line). Here are two pertinent stories for you to consider:

Sally, fifty-five, had been with her husband, Clive, sixty-seven, for almost seventeen years:

"We were work colleagues and had always got on well together but, during a project in Paris, love started to bloom. Clive opened up about the trouble he was having with his daughters and how he was at odds with his wife; I provided a sounding board. On the Eurostar back, he told me that he had feelings for me but I was firm: I didn't want to be his mistress. I thought that was that. A few weeks later, he told me that his marriage was over. We started seeing each other and by that time he'd moved into a hotel and almost immediately found an apartment. I moved in with him a couple of months later. At the time, I thought it was all above board but, looking back, it all happened extremely quickly from Clive declaring his feelings to us living together."

Sally and Clive had a good relationship. They were both very focused on their work and although Sally had never envisioned having children, she enjoyed becoming a stepmother. Everything started to change when Clive wound down toward retirement, left his employer, and took on consultancy work.

"We bought a farmhouse in Normandy and he spent a lot of time doing it up. He wanted me to go part-time too but I still had lots of ambitions left to fulfill," Sally explained.

In effect, they were at different life stages and the strain was beginning to show.

"Clive was very distracted and unpredictable but I put it down to him readjusting to being retired. And then I discovered he was having an affair and, worst of all, he'd taken her to our farmhouse."

Within a fortnight of Sally bringing Clive to therapy to find out if their marriage had a future, he had declared it over, told her he wanted a divorce so he could remarry, and asked for the French farm-house in the settlement.

"I'm beginning to feel that history has repeated itself. He couldn't face the problems in his first marriage and he ran away with me, and now he can't deal with being retired and he's run away with her," Sally reflected.

Moving onto a second example, Arturo and Louise had both left their partners for each other. At the time, Arturo had been fifty and a successful businessman and Louise, who was thirty-three, had worked for him. Ten years later, when they consulted me. Arturo was suffering from Parkinson's disease and had discovered that Louise was friendly with a colleague. They had two young children together and Louise was stressed from working.

"Sometimes it feels like I have three children, not two," Louise complained.

"I do my best to care for the children but my health is compromised," Arturo replied.

"I'm working longer hours because we need the money ..."

"That doesn't make having an affair right," he told her.

"He is just a friend. I need something just for me."

"What sort of friend do you send hundreds of texts to?"

The argument was going round in circles and whether this emotional affair had crossed over into becoming physical had become immaterial. Sally had taken a shortcut to avoid the pain of coping with a partner with a life-threatening illness and two demanding young children. Rather than talking about the problems with Arturo, she had found comfort by talking to someone else.

Key questions: Is this new relationship really a shortcut? It takes a lot of work to have a good divorce and develop better communication skills (to cope with the demands of co-parenting). Would it be better to invest your time and your improved skills in repairing your current relationship? What is the long-term impact of taking a shortcut?

EXERCISE HOW TO FALL OUT OF LOVE

Whether you've become close to someone and aware that you're in danger of crossing over into affair territory, or you're already having an affair and considering ending it, this is how to step back from the brink.

Grieve for the loss

Goodbyes and endings are tough, so expect to be sad and feel down or tearful when you step back—it's all part of the healing process:

- If you're finding it particularly tough, think about other losses in your life, particularly when you were young. Were you told to be strong so as not to upset others?

- Could you be mourning not just the end of this love but other losses too (even a job that you loved or the old you before you had kids)?

- If you find yourself thinking about your lover it doesn't mean you *should* still be together; it's just part of the natural grieving process.

- Don't expect a pain-free ending. Lots of people think if they let go gradually or meet their lover one more time that it will make them feel better. It never works because you can't magic pain away.

Don't feed the pain

It's tempting to wallow from time to time, or even web stalk, but you'll just make it harder for yourself.

- Change the radio station when "our song" comes on.

- Don't walk past where he or she works.

- Don't keep in touch with mutual friends just so you can talk about him or her or hope to hear news.

- Don't stay friends on Facebook or contact them online when you've had a couple of drinks.

Reconnect with your partner

In order to have an affair or for your affections to be so easily captured by someone else, you will have disconnected from your partner. So start to reverse the process now:

- Tell your partner about what happens in your daily life and show a real interest in him or her. Often we get bored because we don't know enough about our partner, or because we think we already know everything there is to know.

- When you're annoyed about something they've said or done, don't ignore it and hold it against your partner—tell them, respectfully.

- Take your partner's side, rather than forming a coalition with one of your children against him or her.

- Be around more and remember to smile when you see your partner.

- If you're not up for sex, you can still have a cuddle in bed or on the couch. Sometimes a touch is worth a thousand words.

- Make your partner a priority in your life.

Identify the underlying problems in your relationship

When someone is sexually or emotionally unfaithful, there are normally longstanding issues that need to be resolved:

- If you don't know off the top of your head what the key issue might be, then think about the subjects that your partner doesn't want to discuss! (It's normally one of those.)

- The most common causes of friction between couples are money, sex, and the division of household chores or childcare. It could be time to review these topics again. What might have worked OK ten years ago is probably out of date today.

- Don't be afraid to ask for outside help like couple counseling.

Communicate effectively

If you can talk and listen to each other, you're halfway to solving even the most intractable problem.

- I summarize good communication as "I can ask, you can say no and we can negotiate."

- Unfortunately, we are frightened of asking in case we don't get it—and prefer to drop hints or expect our partner to somehow know what we really want.

- We're frightened of saying no because we're anxious our partner might not like us—and end up getting overburdened and resentful instead.

- We are not shown how to negotiate at school.

- We unconsciously mirror our parents' behavior, which often doesn't work (like shouting at our partner and then withdrawing).

Consider telling the truth

If the atmosphere is still bad, and you are the one who has been having the affair, you might need to consider making a full confession and removing the secrets from your relationship.

- You think you've been discreet but your partner might have been secretly following every twist in your affair by checking your emails or your cell phone or tracking your car.

- Even if he or she doesn't consciously know about your affair, he or she senses there may be someone else but is afraid to confront that knowledge and is feeling stuck.

- Confession provides a chance to bring everything into the open.

- Your partner might be angry in the short-term but relieved that he or she "wasn't going mad"—because there was a real problem all along.

- It is easy to think that you are protecting your partner, but could you really be protecting yourself from having to deal with your feelings?

- The truth may create two people working on your relationship—rather than just you (or even worse, neither of you!).

TURNING YOUR PARTNER
INTO YOUR SIGNIFICANT OTHER

I was once asked on a radio discussion program what was the craziest thing I'd done for love. They were expecting something extraordinary. (Someone talked about letting his girlfriend run over him in her car, gently, he insisted, during an angry argument about whether he trusted her or not.) In fact, the craziest thing I've done so far was to invite someone I hardly knew into my life and get married to them. I don't think anybody would take such an enormous risk without the magic of limerence and the power of projection.

True love—rather than the crazy stuff they were talking about on that radio show—only happens when we stop believing our partners are the great other and we embrace them in all their complexity, rather than how we might like them to be; when we see them as separate individuals, rather than simply the object of our desire.

So if you can't expect your partner to save you, what can you expect? In my experience, there are six areas where your partner can become your significant other, rather than your great other.

Companionship: Humans are social creatures, and we have a deep-seated desire to be with other people. With a significant other, there's less need to plan ahead because you have someone to, for example, drive up to the nearest hilltop with on a beautiful evening and watch the sun go down. He or she is also a companion for exploring the wider world.

Support: Your partner is not there to carry you through life (like a great other), but he or she can provide a leg-up over a wall or a helping hand across a stream (like a significant other). In other words, expecting your partner to do the work for you is unfair; asking for help and support is fine. For example, your partner cannot take away your pain when your mother or father is dying, but he or she can drive you to the hospital and sit with you by the bedside or have a hot meal waiting when you get home.

Growth: Nobody can challenge you like your partner. Your mother and father may think you're wonderful just the way you are and friends might gently point out your weaknesses, but they don't live with you. It is your partner who can offer a true mirror and a proper challenge. It may not always be pleasant—I love my routines but my partner gently, and sometimes not so gently, pushes me out of my comfort zone. Being challenged (with kindness) is generally in our best interests, especially as we grow older and can become more set in our ways.

Witness: We live in a fast-moving world and it is easy to feel invisible. Of course you can use social media to chart your every move but a great witness for your regular triumphs and disasters is your partner. He or she is also someone with whom to celebrate birthdays, Christmas, and major achievements.

Respect: There is someone in the world who considers your feelings and values them. It might not always be possible to fulfill all your needs but your partner should listen and hopefully will ask: how can I help *you*?

Continuity: I appreciate long-term relationships more and more as I get older. There is a peace that comes with continuity and acceptance of our strengths as well as our weaknesses.

How to achieve this goal

For a relationship to not only put down lasting roots but to keep them watered and fed too, you need to do three things:

Keep talking Friedrich Nietzsche called marriage "the grand dialogue" but a lot of couples have exhausted the conversation because they have stopped growing or are frightened to share their inner thoughts and feelings (or have started telling them only to family, friends, or even a lover). It can sometimes be easier to pretend to be moving along the same path together rather than checking your ideas are in alignment, but when you stop talking and start assuming, you will end up tripping over rather than supporting each other.

Cultivate curiosity: The English essayist, lexicographer, and moralist Samuel Johnson (1709–1784) wrote that "Curiosity is, in great and generous minds, the first passion and the last." Not only does curiosity cultivate interest in our partner (so he or she becomes less of a stranger) but it helps us to stop hearing his or her thoughts and feelings as criticism.

One of the most important questions to ask your partner in the middle passage is: What were your dreams and what has blocked you? Although you may have asked your partner the first question, you may not have asked the second for fear of what you might hear. (Although you imagine the answer will put the blame on you, it's more likely the blockage will be something personal to your partner or circumstances beyond either of your control.) However, if you cultivate curiosity, you are more likely to use the three most powerful words in the English language: not "I love you" but "Tell me more." If you are genuinely curious about what makes your partner tick, the two of you are more likely to keep the grand dialogue alive.

Learn to forgive: The German philosopher Immanuel Kant (1724–1804) is responsible for my favorite saying: "Out of the crooked timber of humanity no straight thing was ever made." (It is the basis for one of my nine maxims in *Wake Up and Change Your Life: How to survive a crisis and be stronger, wiser, and happier.*) If we forgive our partner for being "crooked timber" (and therefore not the great other), there is a chance that he or she will forgive our crookedness too. There is another benefit: you might start to forgive yourself for not being perfect and that's a great asset when you are taking stock in your forties and fifties and preparing for the next phase of your life. With forgiveness, you have a route back to the grand dialogue when something goes wrong.

YOU'RE NOT ALONE

The myth of the Great Other is so strong (from fairy-tales and superhero movies) that it is hard to accept that he or she will not rescue us. There is a small child inside all of us who longs for the perfect mommy or daddy to come along and make everything better—especially if we didn't have enough parenting when we were young. No wonder we stamp our feet and find the invitation to cross from provisional adult (the first half) into full adulthood (second half) so difficult. However, once you give up the idea of the great other, it is easier to recognize the value of good companions that you meet along the way during your journey through life. They could be friends, work mates, or someone who provides a piece of the jigsaw for the existential questions of the middle passage. (These are: Who am I? What gives my life meaning? What are my values?) My affair was damaging for all three of us caught up in the triangle, but my lover (a) introduced me to meditation and (b) taught me that I had transgressed my core values and by pretending that my actions did not have consequences, I was only fooling myself.

Although there is no guru with all the answers, there is valuable knowledge to be gleaned from wise men and women whose wisdom has resonated across the centuries. I am currently reading *Tao Te Ching*, one of the world's oldest and most profound literary treasures, written by Lao Tzu (whose name means old master) 2,500 years ago in China. It comprises eighty-one brief but enigmatic verses that still speak to us today. For example:

"When we try and control the future,
  we are like an inexperienced child
  trying to take the place
  of the master carpenter.

When you try to handle the blade
  of a master carpenter,
  chances are you will cut your hand."

In this book I have drawn on Nietzsche, Kant, Montaigne, and Dr. Johnson, and in previous writings I have been influenced by the ancient Greek philosophers like Aristotle, Pythagoras, and Epictetus. There are contemporary writers whose work feeds my thoughts. (See the further reading section.) Although I am tempted to describe some of these thinkers (both from past and present) as my mentors or gurus, I resist the idea because it always leads to disappointment.

For instance, I have always admired the writer Jeanette Winterson (author of *Oranges Are Not the Only Fruit* and *Why be Happy When You Can Be Normal*), not just for her extraordinary creativity but for how her wisdom shines through in interviews. So when she gave a lecture at my local literary festival, I dropped everything to be there. It was an engaging hour but, of course, she did not have all the answers (because she's not the great other). She has thought deeply about identity and the big questions of life and I can benefit from her insights. But ultimately, it is up to each of us to piece together *our* truth, not to simply adopt someone else's. Hopefully, my books can be a resource on your journey.

Finally, even though there is no great other, there is someone else, someone key, whom I haven't discussed yet. So who is it? James Hollis puts it particularly eloquently:

"There is no one out there to save us, to take care of us, to heal the hurt. But there is a very fine person within, one we barely know ready and willing to be our constant companion."

The great advantage of being forty- or fifty-something is that you are finally ready to meet them.

SUMMING UP

➤ The myth of the great other—who will save us and make our life meaningful—is extremely powerful.

➤ We are particularly prone to affairs in our middle years because they seem to provide a shortcut to feeling better and easing the work of the middle passage.

➤ Once you stop setting your partner up to be something he or she cannot be (and getting angry about their failure), you can begin to recognize the strengths of the relationship that you do share.

CHAPTER FIVE

Turning your life around

Whether the plan for your life has been conscious (with a number of specific life-goals) or largely spontaneous (an unarticulated search for the good life), it doesn't seem to be working any more. When faced with the inevitable disappointment, confusion, and anger that can come from feeling stuck or lost, it is natural to try a combination of the following approaches:

1. *Denial.* It is simply impossible that life has brought me to this juncture. There must be some mistake and if I keep my head down, something will click into place and I'll be back on track again.

2. *Revive efforts in service of the old plan.* If the plan isn't working, because I can no longer ignore the evidence of my own eyes I must be doing something wrong. I need to work harder, longer, or find ways to bend others to suit my plan.

3. *Bring on the coping mechanisms.* In many ways this is a combination of the first two approaches: I will manage my unhappiness (while waiting for the great other) by self-medicating (with drink, pre-scription drugs, street drugs, computer games, pornography, flirting

with a stranger or a work colleague, compulsive shopping, etc.). Alternatively, I will manage the pain of trying to make the old plan fit with distractions (like TV, nights out, social media, mindless hedonism).

4. *Find a new incarnation of the old plan.* My goals are fine. The problem is that I took the wrong path to fulfill my needs for more money, more possessions, more success, and more praise.

Alternatively, you could listen to the quiet voice that is saying: "There's got to be a better way." The key here is *what worked in the first part of your life will probably not work in the second.* Rather than rushing ahead with yet another failed approach, you need to stop and take stock. Instead of focusing on *external* matters, it's time to switch to the *internal* and meet your true self.

It may sound daunting but in this chapter I will prepare you for this appointment, help you put together a well-made plan for the second half of your life and provide skills to communicate better with your partner and family (so they are more likely to buy into your plan). First, I want to offer a little reassurance.

WHY MIDLIFE IS THE PERFECT TIME FOR AN APPOINTMENT WITH YOUR TRUE SELF

You've probably no idea who you are—beyond your roles of partner, parent, provider, homemaker, etc. If you're honest, you're feeling anxious about meeting your true self. If you were like me in my late thirties, you'd rather retreat into the certainties of your old life. But now, changing circumstances—in my case, my partner's terminal illness and my chosen industry going through a period of huge upheaval—are making that impossible. Perhaps you don't really like yourself much or you've been doing things that make you feel ashamed. Once again, I understand those feelings because I struggled with them myself. Yet however much we might kick against the idea, being forty- or fifty-something is the ideal time to meet our true self:

- We have plenty of personal history from which to learn.

- We have developed some emotional resilience and know from experience that we can survive a crisis.

- We have more insight into what works and what doesn't work for us.

- We have built up more resources and therefore have more choices.

- We are becoming aware that there is a ticking clock—a great motivator.

- We still have enough time and energy to change.

If you're still anxious, ask yourself this question: If not now, when?

JOB VERSUS VOCATION

Perhaps the best place to start is your job. We spend so much of our time at work and it provides status (from both our colleagues and the wider world), money (to buy the trappings of success), and a way of measuring ourselves against others (to bolster our ego). Except these are all *external* factors and the task for the second half of life is internal: Does your job feed you or does your work seem rather pointless (beyond the pay check that keeps a roof over your heads and feeds the family)?

What is a job?

A job is work that earns money and, if you are lucky, meets your needs (for belonging, appreciation, and self-respect). Unfortunately, at school, and maybe later at college too, you were categorized by what you were good at rather than what you felt driven by or even called to do. The further you climbed up the ladder, the more focused you needed to become—often on the next rung—and the narrower your outlook became. (It is extremely rare to be taken into a company and given the chance to try out every department and choose what interests you most.) You are likely to have followed a path into greater specialization. If you trained in law, perhaps you focused on maritime law and then cargo compensation cases—and maybe only for one product. Specialization is easier because it is what everyone expects in the job market, and the work then becomes easier too because you can carry knowledge over from one project to another (without having to start from scratch each time). Unfortunately, there is a downside:

You neglect the full person: We have four basic ways of approaching the world. These are *thinking* (looking logically at a problem), *feeling* (considering the emotional impact of a decision), *sensation* (working with your hands to sculpt, craft, cook, etc. or using your body to lift, run, or jump), and *intuition* (searching for deeper truths). Does your job feed each of these functions?

Someone else is defining success: A combination of technology (which makes it easier for employers to centralize decision-making and monitor staff) and the triumph of neoliberal thinking (which focuses on ranking and competing) has created a very narrow definition of success. To take an example from a law firm, it is not about the complexity of the case or winning against the odds or even client satisfaction, but how many hours are billed that is truly valued—in comparison with your colleagues and your own performance last year. Even professions that don't have ready-made statistics have them imposed. For example, a hospital's success will partly be measured by waiting times. Pretty soon if something about your job can't be measured, it will be downgraded. Has your job been drained of its original meaning and your attention focused on arbitrary targets or, even worse, have you felt duty-bound to manipulate the system to meet these goals?

Anxiety: You are only as good as your last result. Some companies even follow a policy called "rank and yank" where the top performers get bonuses and the bottom 10 percent are fired. Your whole industry might undergo what is euphemistically called restructuring and your job might disappear or be transferred to the other side of the world. Men in particular are conditioned to think of themselves as synonymous with their work and their main identity as being provider. How does anxiety about job security impact on your daily life?

Example: Simon, fifty-five, had spent most of his career in the oil business, but the slump in prices in 2015 meant that his employers were looking to make savings and streamline staff.

"I've always liked my job because I was recruited to think outside the box and I always felt that I could add value to everything that I did," he told me. "At the moment, we have a team from head office looking into how we operate. I'd be fine if they were genuinely interested in doing things better, but in reality they want to knock 20 percent off our costs. I was talking to one of my colleagues who joked: 'Of course they can have 20 percent off the project. I found them their saving at a stroke—look, everything's suddenly cheaper. Except we know how much oil exploration really costs.' In other words, the project will eventually overrun the new budget and the company will have to pick up the bill further down the line. In the meantime, everybody is happy—except me, because I feel a fraud."

What is a vocation?

There is a lot of advice around on how to be more successful at work but precious little about how to make our work more meaningful. That's why I particularly like this quote from Frederick Buechner, an American writer and theologian: "At what points do my talents and deep gladness meet the world's deep need?" While you choose a job or a career, a vocation chooses you. So how do you know the difference? With a vocation, or a calling, your life would be unrecognizable unless you pursued this line of activity. Unlike a job, there is no downside to a vocation.

Taps into your potential: Don't worry if your vocation is not obvious. Trust me, you are full of potential but may not know your full extent yet. Perhaps your teachers cultivated your most obvious talents (like obedience or passing exams) and sent you down the wrong path. Perhaps your school and friends valued skills that you did not possess (for example kicking a ball around) and you did not learn to value yourself. Alternatively, you did not blossom to society's current timetables—not being ready or prepared for exams at eleven, sixteen, eighteen, or twenty-one.

Fortunately it's never too late to discover your talents, your "deep gladness" (or passion) or the world's "deep need." What you love to do may have changed since you were in your teens and twenties.

Personal autonomy: Instead of trying to be successful by meeting other people's goals or expectations, you are serving the task itself. If you were a carpenter, you would focus on creating a beautiful piece of furniture that first met your own criteria for beauty and functionality. Of course, your designs might not be fashionable or more people might want chairs than the cabinets that you create. In that instance, chairs could be someone else's vocation and rather than bend to other people's will, you could remain true to your calling to make cabinets.

Most probably, your work draws on a variety of different skills. What do you find satisfying about your job? What parts feed you? What is your central task? How can you serve your needs without being distracted by the meetings, targets, and administration that surround it? What would happen if you judged your efforts against your own values rather than everybody else's? You need to consider your employer's goals in order to keep your job, but you don't have to buy into their values to the extent that you dismiss your own.

Integrity: Instead of comparing yourself to other people and becoming envious of their achievements, try measuring your actions against your own values. I love the quote from Henry David Thoreau:

"If a man does not keep pace with his companions, perhaps it is because he hears a different drummer. Let him step to the music which he hears, however measured or far away."

In this way, you are less likely to act in ways that are morally questionable or fight against your calling. I had a friend whose vocation was teaching but he was between contracts:

"I really needed money so I took a job in a call center where I had to phone people and sell products. It was heart-destroying because I spent all day getting knockbacks or making people angry. The staff was divided into two teams in two rooms and we competed against each other for prizes. One week, we won having a sound system installed and loud music played." My friend was a gentle soul. "It went thud, thud, thud, all day. How could they stand it? After two weeks I became ill, and lying at home I realized something important: I didn't need the money that much."

If you're feeling uncomfortable about some part of your work, it is important to stop and ask yourself: What is my feeling trying to tell me? It could be that your integrity has been compromised and this is a sure sign that you've strayed from your path (or been pushed off it).

Example: I think we get a call many times before finally finding our vocation. In the nineties, it was difficult to decide if I'd had enough of working in radio or if radio had had enough of me. I blush when I think back to my thirty-something self: I had decided that if I became famous all doors would open to me and I could do whatever I liked. It didn't occur to me to work out what interested me first and pursue that! In the meantime, I began to use some of the skills that I'd abandoned as I rose up the management ladder in radio and returned to journalism (but switched across to newspapers and magazines). Oddly, I didn't think to use my experience as a marital therapist until editors started asking for pieces about relationships. An agent suggested I turn one of my articles into a book (which became the international bestseller *I Love You But I'm Not in Love With You*). It took a couple of books and a reader telling me it "must be really satisfying to know your life purpose" before it finally clicked. My vocation was writing and teaching!

Once you've found your vocation, it is amazing how everything can start falling into place. If I was still in the first half of my life (chasing fame, money, and wanting my ego stroked) I might have been tempted to write about something other than relationships that would potentially appeal to a wider audience. In the second half of life, I would rather be true to my calling: explaining what I know about the complexity of relationships and teaching the skills for dealing with them.

What if I don't have a vocation?

You may be thinking that it's all very well for people who are creative (and can hold the fruits of their labor) or who help others (and can see the results of their efforts), but your own work is not so straightforward. Perhaps there is no end product that you can hold in your hands. You feel like a small part of a large organization, your work is made up of lots of different tasks, or it is very administrative. Maybe you hate your job but your family love eating and having a roof over their head. So how can you possibly find your vocation?

Listen: It is perfectly possible that you have been called to do something different but you have covered your eyes or dismissed the thought with lots of practical obstacles. If you let the idea develop or discuss it with people that you respect, the problems might not be overwhelming. Alternatively, finding something in a similar field might work better for you. The next time you have an idea let it brew, and if someone offers to open a door, look through it.

Give yourself time: We live in an instant society that believes in natural talent. Anders Ericsson, a professor at the University of Colorado, wrote that it took, on average, 10,000 hours to become truly proficient at something. He used a study of German children who played the violin from 5 to 20 years old and he found that the elite had averaged 10,000 hours of practice and the less able only 4,000. So don't be downcast if your new interests do not immediately translate into proficiency; if you have the passion, the maturity to keep going, and a real calling, you will get there. In the meantime, give yourself permission to take time, develop contacts, and find your niche.

If your passion is something you do part-time, alongside work, or in snatched hours here and there, that is fine. You are actually doing it. This is better than relying on magical, heroic, or wishful thinking to make it happen.

Get things wrong: In the job world, we are terrified of getting things wrong because it could lead to some form of punishment or even dismissal. In your middle years, you can begin to look past terms like success and failure because you can learn a lot from your mistakes. Success can entrap you into doing the same thing and make experimentation harder. During the middle passage, you need to discover your own values and judge for yourself what is right or wrong for you. Nobody finds their vocation without first getting things wrong.

Beware of salespeople: Their job is to make you feel that you don't have enough money, success, or status already. In effect, they are trying to encourage you to think first half rather than second half of life.

It's not all about the money: Of course you need a certain level of income but what would your family rather have: expensive vacations, consumer goodies, and an angry provider who is leaking resentment, or a happy and content person doing less expensive things with them? If in doubt, ask your partner and, if they're old enough, your children too. The other idea I want to plant is that *you don't have to be paid for your passion.* It could be that your calling does not make money (at least in the short- or medium-term). You might want to go surfing or play the guitar and if those few hours each week are what gives your life meaning rather than your job, that's fine.

Your ultimate vocation is to become yourself: You don't have to leave your job to find yourself but it would help if you made your work more satisfying. Which parts of your job do you find most rewarding? How could you focus on those? Which parts do you find most alienating? How could you spend less time and psychological energy on those areas? In a nutshell, think: How could I work differently? How could my job better match who I am?

Example: Ben, fifty-seven, came to see me because, in his words, "My life is a bit rubbish." He didn't know if it was because his marriage had lost its shine or "because I'm grumpy and dissatisfied with everything." I suggested that we look at his marriage first and he started couple counseling with his wife. I helped them discuss issues that they had previously buried and to improve communication. About eighteen months later he came back: although his marriage was "as good as it's going to get" he was still disappointed by life.

"I think the problem is me," he concluded.

So I helped Ben to live more in the moment and less in the future (using mindfulness), took him through my personal development program (outlined in *Wake Up and Change Your Life*), and we discussed the U-shaped life and the middle passage.

"I have developed a good business and employ a good team but I don't feel passionate about it any more," he said. "Sometimes it feels like I'm working to provide my staff with good jobs more than anything else."

"You're working for them, rather than them for you?" I asked.

Ben laughed:

"You've hit the nail on the head."

So we talked about what did provide meaning: his children (from his current marriage) and his children and grandchildren (from his first marriage).

"I would like to wind down, maybe even retire, but with two children under twelve that's not really practical."

"So how could you work differently so you spend more time at home and less at work?"

This question provided the breakthrough.

The next week, Ben returned to see me with a big smile on his face.

"I've taken back control of my office diary There are times when customers need to see me and nobody else will do. However, my staff had booked me into see somebody across the other side of town on Friday afternoon and by the time I'd fought my way back past through the end-of-the-week traffic I wouldn't have finished until seven. They had also scheduled me to make a hundred mile journey for a meeting with another client. On previous occasions, I would have just gritted my teeth and gone along with the plan—and probably been in a foul mood. However, as I thought, the customer on Friday afternoon could bring the appointment forward to the morning and the one who involved the long round trip could wait until I had two appointments in the area—thus making the trip more worthwhile.'

What next? The careers advice given to people considering a midlife career change and the task of the middle passage are the same: understand your priorities and your needs. So the good news is that you have already started on this task.

If you have no ideas or are unsure about the next step, consider taking a test or questionnaire. Career counselors have a variety of tools that could quick start your thinking, or look for a self-assessment test online.

Talk to your friends, in particular those who knew you at important points on your journey. For example, discussing your dilemma with someone who knew you at college will bring a fresh perspective and maybe remind you of interests or talents that you have overlooked.

Look for a way to take your existing skills into a new area, for example I knew a nurse who trained to become a barrister specializing in medical negligence cases.

Finally, test the waters. The best way to discover if something is truly right is to experience it first-hand. You could so some voluntary work or a low-paid entry job in that field (before signing up for an expensive degree) to see if the work still interests you.

HOW TO BECOME YOURSELF

Once you have become aware of the influence of other people on your life and the impact of your job, you are ready to start to ask the most important question of the middle passage: Who am I? So where do you start?

Embrace solitude

To understand yourself properly, you need to be wholly present. That's a difficult concept to get your head around. Nietzsche writes: "When we are alone and quiet we are afraid that something will be whispered in our ear, and so we hate the silence and drug ourselves with social life." For example, as I write this, my partner is away working. This morning, I thought: "The house is too quiet." So I put the radio on for some music, but within a few minutes I was thinking about a news item that had been broadcast, and the possibility to meet myself (and my *own* thoughts and feelings rather than the opinions and outrage of others) had slipped away.

How to achieve it: It is OK to take time out of your day and do nothing. In the words of the Welsh poet William Henry Davies (1871–1940): "What is this life, if, full of care, we have no time to stand and stare." Davies, who spent a significant amount of his life as a tramp in both the UK and US, concludes in his famous poem that it would be a poor life. So what would happen if you put away your everyday distractions and switched off the TV, radio, or phone? What might you learn about yourself or about life? One of my clients sat on a bench and watched everyone go past: "They seemed like zombies rushing to nowhere particularly important, in the greater scheme of things, and then it hit me: I spend the majority of my time doing exactly the same."

Aim for an adult relationship with your parents

The task at adolescence and young adulthood is to separate from your parents and to leave home; the task in your middle years is to separate from their earlier ambitions and expectations for you. This is particularly difficult for two reasons. First, your parents' wishes reinforce your provisional adulthood identity. Let me explain by giving an example.

Christopher, fifty-two, did not think his office stationery business was successful enough, and his main rival was making more money (even though Christopher's products were better). I saw a man who was successful enough to live abroad for large chunks of the year and eat in the best restaurants. I wondered what messages he had received from his parents and how much they had encouraged him to build tall towers to his (and most probably their) greater glory.

"My mother didn't have a particular plan," he said, "but she told me loud and clear that I had to do something 'remarkable' with my life." So Christopher's provisional identity had been to be remarkable. To this end he worked in various countries with NGOs trying to make a difference, which later led him to become a businessman. But neither of these roles was right for Christopher and during our counseling he revealed that what he really wanted to do was to write. So what had been stopping him? "I didn't think I could be successful or remarkable enough at it," he replied.

Another category who have trouble separating from their parents' ambitions or expectations are those who were desperate for their parents' love. Geoffrey, also fifty-two, remembered his mother's overriding message to "run along and play" and his father only being interested in him as "the dutiful son who would go into the family business." During our counseling sessions he often asked my permission to, for example, watch half an hour of pornography or to side-step discussing his marriage (which had just broken down) on a first date. As you can imagine, my job is not to be a stand-in authority figure giving a thumbs up or thumbs down (and I believe Geoffrey is the best judge of what he should do). However, I could help him find his own authority—rather than bowing to his parents or parent substitutes—and break free from his childhood issues. I knew we were making progress when he kept on saying, "I don't need to ask permission to ..."

How to achieve it: If you find yourself regressing back to childhood when you step through your parents' door, have problems dealing with surrogate authority figures, or have internal arguments with a judgmental voice inside your own head, you may find the idea of

Transactional Analysis (TA), a theory developed in the 1950s, really useful. In a nutshell, we have three different modes of being: parent, adult, and child. The definitions of these in Transactional Analysis are slightly different from how we commonly understand them.

Parent is divided into two halves: critical and nurturing. Child is also divided into two halves: free (when you are being creative, intuitive, and having fun) and adapted (when you are relating to others by being people-pleasing, rebelling, defensive, playing the martyr, adopting passive-aggressive behavior, sulking, closing down, throwing a tantrum, and so on). The adult mode is all about problem-solving. It asks who, what, why, when? It stays in the present—rather than throwing in examples from the past (which is critical parent)—and it is assertive and equally prepared to listen as to speak. There is no ideal place to be because we need both parts in our personality. The problem comes when we get stuck in one particular way of being.

The other central idea of Transactional Analysis is that our mode of being will influence which one other people adopt. The most common combination is parent (critical) and child (adapted), although I see lots of smothering parents (nurturing) and appeasing children (adapted)—particularly from sons who will do anything for their mothers (even if that includes watching her run down his wife). However, you can have an adult to adult relationship with your parents. So how does this work?

So if your parents start to treat you like a child, don't get critical yourself (and go into critical parent mode) or regress into your standard adapted child behavior; instead go into adult and ask them a question: "Why is this important to you? You seem angry/upset/fed up. What is really the matter?" Equally if one of your parent's health is seriously compromised, it is tempting to want to take charge. However, you would be stepping into nurturing parent and they would respond as adapted child. Stay in adult and ask a question: "What are the options?"

It might take time and patience but I promise if you stay in adult mode with your parents, they will join you in adult too. (There is more about TA in the second part of this book.)

Connect with your lost child

Many people are bored with life (and themselves and their partners) in their forties and fifties because their lives have become too narrowly channeled—and, in effect, dammed up. The narrowing could have come from too much specialization in their work, meaning some talent or interest is no longer being explored, or because the responsibilities of being a parent mean there is not enough time for hobbies. Maybe they left something important behind when they crossed over from being a child to a teenager. It might be a sense of wonder about the world—not cool when we become teenagers. Perhaps they were never properly a child.

Armando, forty, was a lawyer who told me to google him (so I had some idea of how successful he was). During our work together, he told me how he felt when he was ten:

"I remembered thinking how important it was to get into law school on the first attempt and what I needed to do to be in pole position—because if I failed at eighteen, and had to wait another year, that would mean that I would not be fully qualified until twenty-four. I never took anything for granted." I doubt he had much time to play or find out his other qualities—beyond being driven. But we need to know all facets of ourselves to discover who we are in the middle passage.

How to achieve it: I want to focus on the free child of Transactional Analysis. This is the creative and intuitive part of ourselves that is often squashed as we get older and "put away childish things." In fact, we need our childish curiosity about the world and, most importantly, we still need to play even when we are adults.

So what might you do? It could be something creative (taking up singing or buying an adult coloring book) or in the great outdoors (hiking or white-water rafting) or doing something with your hands (working a lathe or baking bread), but it is important that you escape your normal environment and have fun. Whenever I run workshops, I get everybody to play a party game (like blind man's buff or musical chairs) as it knocks down barriers and energizes the group.

When you have played, or been silly, ask yourself: What part of myself have I put aside?

Take back the projection

There are two types of projection: positive (where we put all our faith and hope in someone else) and negative (where we recognize the things that we dislike about ourselves in someone else, and distance ourselves from that person by criticizing or policing their behavior).

Starting with the positive, it is important to acknowledge our disappointment that there is no great other to save us, and to discover the upside of letting go of this fantasy. In my first relationship, my partner did most of the cooking when we entertained. In the first year of mourning, I was unable to have friends round for a meal because I felt completely deskilled. It took me quite a while to rediscover my own culinary achievements—and take back my projections—but I realized that I had played down my abilities in order to make my partner feel valued as the chef of the family.

Moving onto negative projection, I find the best way to explain this is by talking about something called "queer bashing." This is where a group of young men assault someone openly gay. As you can imagine, most heterosexuals do not need to "prove" themselves by shouting insults, acting aggressively, and "teaching" gay or lesbian people "a lesson." In effect, these youths are disowning their own same sex attraction or their feminine characteristics, by recognizing those qualities in someone else and attacking them. For most of us, the negative projections we experience are not so dramatic. If, for example, you dislike somebody at work for being a know-it-all, have you ever lacked humility yourself? If you get annoyed because someone you know thinks only of him or herself, have you ever been accused of being selfish? If you have criticized someone for being needy, were you just distancing yourself from your own inner neediness? It is always easier to take the speck out of someone else's eye than the plank out of our own. If you stop negatively projecting onto others, you will have more energy to invest in becoming yourself.

How to achieve it: For the next week, I'd like you keep a note of your projections. If you have a strong reaction to someone or something, jot the feeling or incident down and spend a couple of minutes looking for the projection. It could be that you've just recognized in someone else something that you don't like about yourself.

If you feel someone has let you down, could it be because you've expected them to assume responsibility for your well-being? Is your response far greater than the offence merited? (For example, anger rather than disappointment.) I'd also like you to look out for over-the-top reactions from other people. Maybe they are projecting something onto you: both positive and negative.

Finally, think about the roles that other people have come to expect from you: like being the nurturer or the provider. What would happen if you let this mantle of responsibility go? Could you start to nurture yourself instead of providing for everybody else (and getting angry when they don't fulfill your needs in return)?

At the end of the week, go back over your diary and reflect on what you've learned about yourself.

Face your shadow

Like lots of my clients, Geoffrey, whom we met earlier, claimed to bury bad experiences and uncomfortable feelings: "If something is overwhelming, and I can't change it, I imagine putting it in a lead-lined box, burying it in the ground, and forgetting it." It is a powerful image but I think an unhelpful one. I prefer an idea from Jung. He believed that the parts of us that we consciously or unconsciously disown are carried around in our shadow.

"So what happens to things we cast into the shadows?" I asked Geoffrey after explaining Jung's concept.

"They become even more frightening," he said.

"But if we turn on the light and look under the bed or behind the door?"

"It's not quite so frightening."

So what would happen if you faced your shadow? First off, you would be more conscious of projection because the negative projections are all about your disowned parts. Even positive projections are fed by the shadow because your need—and everybody else's—to have someone else to "fix" you goes back to your childhood feeling of being inadequate (after all the world is big and dangerous and you were small) or monstrous (because as a child you would believe that you were as you were treated—so if one of your parents was not loving you would conclude that you were unlovable). Secondly, what would happen if you faced your shadow? You could accept that everybody is made up of light and dark qualities and although nobody likes admitting it, humans are full of inconsistencies. We have strengths and weaknesses, and are capable of love and hate, generosity and selfishness, hard work, and being lazy. If you are going to know yourself, you have to own all the parts of yourself. Becoming a full adult involves a move from being fragmented (for example, acting one way at work and one way at home) to being more whole (and facing your shadows).

How to achieve it: I love the quote from Dr. Samuel Johnson: "A man of genius has been seldom ruined but by himself." Johnson was very much a divided man. He spent a lot of his time in taverns but he also created the first English dictionary in just eight years (with the help of six clerks) while the French Academy achieved the same task in fifty years (using forty scholars). He was both melancholic and humorous, full of common sense, and irrational, comforted yet tormented by religion, and he considered his imagination something to be treasured and feared (as he suffered from nighttime terrors). What I'm trying to say is: don't be afraid of your shadow. Not only is nothing quite so bad when we stop and look at it calmly, but what we consider to be weakness could be necessary (laziness can replenish your batteries) and what we consider a virtue might cause problems (working hard can tip into workaholism). We grow and learn about ourselves by confronting our contradictions—rather than casting them into the shadows.

In his 2015 book *The Road to Character,* the *New Yorker* columnist and bestselling author David Brooks draws on the lives of over a dozen outstanding people from history, like Dr. Johnson, who became successful or lived a morally rounded life by confronting their divided natures. It is really reassuring to discover that most of these characters did not achieve greatness until the second half of their lives. One of Brooks' central points is that wisdom comes from admitting our ignorance. He believes we can't see the complex web that causes or drives the big events in our lives, and we can't grasp the depths of our minds, but we can draw on the knowledge of others accumulated over time. His book provides plenty of evidence to show that facing the parts of ourselves we don't like eventually leads to a more meaningful life.

So look around at the people you admire: what makes them special? Read a biography and look for contradictions in his or her character. How aware of his or her divided self was your idol? What impact did this awareness (or lack of it) have on the trajectory of his or her life? What can you learn from these people for your journey?

Aim for the passionate life

There is a level of intelligence far greater than our day-to-day thoughts, and to reach it you need to dive beneath the surface ripples of your mind. How do you achieve that?

When you are doing something that you feel passionate about, your consciousness will begin to expand. Joseph Campbell sums the idea up with "follow your bliss," and he's right, because a life without passion is a life without depth. In other words, doing something you feel passionate about will help you to find your life purpose.

Geoffrey was passionate about sailing but found it hard to understand how that could lead to a meaningful life. So I got him talking about it.

"Sailing is not about taking unnecessary risks, but challenging myself to solve and overcome problems: tides, winds, sandbanks," he said. "I'm up against the elements and aware of my smallness in the wider world."

"There is a spiritual dimension to your sailing?" I asked.

"It would have felt odd saying it, but you're right."

Geoffrey had acknowledged an important truth about the universe and his place in it. When we are young, we wrongly imagine ourselves to be the center of the world. During the middle passage, we discover an appropriate place in the universe for ourselves (rather than a deluded one). At first sight, this idea is rather dispiriting but there is an important upside to not being the center, and therefore in control, of the universe. When something goes wrong it is not entirely your fault and everything is not conspiring against you.

When your conscious mind is preoccupied with something engrossing, ideas and solutions can bubble up from your unconscious. My writing career didn't take off until I had my first puppy. Walking Flash provided time out of my daily routine, being in nature was refreshing, and suddenly ideas for plays and books would pop into my mind. The popular US author Stephen King puts it best in his book *On Writing*. He knows when a plot has been delivered to the basement (his subconscious) and when he's ready, he can go downstairs, open up the boxes, and bring the contents upstairs (to his conscious mind) and assemble the story. So while you're doing something that you feel passionate about, an idea or some revelation about yourself could be delivered to your mental basement.

Doing something that you feel passionate about could be a gateway to your new vocation and a more balanced life that feeds not just your external needs, but your internal ones too.

How to achieve it: Instant gratification and immediate results are very much the focus of our fast-paced modern society. These messages are particularly powerful because they chime with our need in the first half of our life to get ourselves established. However, they can easily derail us in the second half.

Jacob, fifty-four, had recently sold his business and retired early. It should have been a great time for him but he had been unsettled by losing his purpose, status, and seniority and was unsure how to structure his day—except when he was going through his bucket-list of exotic vacation destinations. At the same time, his wife, Molly, fifty-three, was preoccupied with her mother (who was dying of cancer) and her father (who was overwhelmed by the impending loss). Not surprisingly, she had less time for Jacob and her interest in sex had dramatically declined.

For some reason, Jacob thought he was following his bliss when he booked a session at a massage parlor, but when Molly found out, his life was engulfed by crisis.

"It's not that he fell in love with someone else, which I could sort of understand, but he deliberately picked up the phone, made the booking, walked through the door, and took off his clothes. Where was his love and concern for me in this process?"

Molly explained why, for her, this betrayal was greater than an affair.

When looking into the pluses of his retirement, Jacob had written down: "Time to do stuff with Molly, time to enjoy our lovely home, time with the kids before they fly the nest, time to help my parents, and time to visit my brother."

I was struck by how much his values were all around the family.

"You're right. Family is incredibly important to me," Jacob confirmed.

"Except you put everything in jeopardy by visiting the massage parlor. You could lose your home and wife and spend less time with the children if you got divorced."

"I know and that's why my actions don't make any sense to me," he said.

An important part of our work, beyond repairing the marriage, was helping Jacob learn about himself and be more fully conscious about his motivations. He had fallen into a common trap by doing something that he appeared to feel passionate about. Of course an orgasm does provide a few moments of bliss, but how long did it last after Jacob put his clothes back on and walked out of the massage parlor?

"Not very long," he said. "When I look back it was rather an empty experience as the woman was pretending she was interested in me and of course I wasn't interested in her after it was over. In reality, I couldn't get out of there quickly enough. I also felt guilty and ashamed."

"Not enough to stop you doing it again," chimed in Molly.

Even six months after discovery, the feelings in my counseling room were raw and uncomfortable.

So how do you know if something is instant gratification rather than true bliss or whether you are genuinely aiming for the passionate life? The crucial test is: do my actions go against my values?

EXERCISE WHO AM I?

It's time to make a first stab at answering the question at the center of the U-shaped life. Don't worry if you find this hard. Even the simple act of *trying* to define yourself is a step in the right direction.

1. Start off by listing any and every possible answer to the question "Who am I?" When I did this exercise myself, I found the following headings helpful:

   External (For example, job, marital status, where you live, ethnic background, etc.)

   Interests (For example, I put "I am a dog owner" and "I am a reader." Others might put "I am a Chicago Bear or Los Angeles Dodgers supporter")

   Qualities (I put "I am compassionate" and "I am a campaigner")

2. When you have at least ten items on your list, go back over them and see if there is anything that seems to describe what the British pediatrician and psychoanalyst Donald Winnicott (1896–1971) called your false self. By this he means the masks that you wear or your compliance with other people's expectations. Write these on a separate piece of paper.

3. Put all the answers in order, starting with the most important elements of your identity and working down to the least important.

You might decide to leave off old items or they might still be part of your jigsaw. Remember, there is no right or wrong answer. It is what makes sense for you rather than for other people. For example, I put "I am a man" sixth on my list. It is probably the first thing other people see but it's not the most important role to me.

TIME IS RUNNING OUT

It can happen at any age but in your forties and fifties, you begin to face up to the truth: nobody is going to live forever. Some of your friends and contemporaries begin to die from what is euphemistically called "natural causes." Your parents start to falter, becoming more dependent on you. The safety buffer between you and the grim reaper is collapsing. At work, you may feel passed over for newer, younger blood, or you can feel your peers breathing down your neck. You don't feel as strong, as attractive, as clever, or whatever else used to define you. Unfortunately, our culture worships youth and novelty. No wonder there are times when you are gripped with panic!

There is a positive way to consider what it means to be mortal: a *time limit helps.* James Hollis captured this idea when he wrote in his book *The Middle Passage:* "If we were immortal, nothing would matter, nothing would really count. But we are not immortal, so each choice matters." So if there are advantages to time running out, what could they be?

Stops you going down blind alleys

If you are capable, there are probably lots of jobs that you could do—but that does not make them right for you. In my midthirties, I was offered some work in market research and went onto to study and get my Market Research Society diploma. Twenty plus years later, I look back on this period of my life with amazement. Why did I waste all that energy and study time on something that didn't really interest me? I know my thirty-something self was worried about paying the mortgage and propping up my radio career. In other words, I was busy building another tall tower to make me look good to outsiders.

Let me give you another example. When I'm working with couples to improve their sex life together, I am frequently reminded how uncomfortable many women feel about their bodies (and what a hindrance that can be to getting naked and relaxing into the intimacy of lovemaking). From time to time, I think I should write a book about women's body image but I remind myself that I have a limited time on earth and that's not my calling (and it would probably be more powerful written by a woman).

I have another example of how a limit concentrates the mind. Recently, I listed the novels I've read on the recommendation of the Goodreads website. At the end of the first year, I had read about twenty. If I live for another twenty-five years, it means I will have only enough time to read *five hundred* books. At first, I was appalled (because every week the book review pages are full of interesting titles and there's lots of authors who I admire but I've only read a couple of their titles), but this exercise gave me a different perspective. In the past, I read *Fifty Shades of Grey* and *The Da Vinci Code* just to see what everybody was talking about and I'm not going to make the same mistake again. Now I read the authors that I'd always been going to get around to but never had—like Tolstoy. And yet, when reading *Anna Karenina*, I had no compunction in skipping the sections that didn't interest me (like the ones about Russian peasant farming methods). Could a similar attitude help you to make the most of your precious time?

Helps you find what is truly important

Bill Clegg was a successful New York literary agent with a glittering career but he felt a fraud on the inside (and managed the contradictions with crack cocaine). He has written about his addiction and how he tried to kill himself during an extended drug and alcohol binge in *Portrait of an Addict as a Young Man* and his recovery and relapses in *Ninety Days*. He is now sober and in his forties and in a recent radio interview to promote his first novel said:

> "My father died this summer and although he lived a full life, I had this overwhelming sense that as we go, we want to start back right away. Not only is life hard but it goes so quickly and so the pleasures are about how we're connected to other people and how we can be useful. It was a surprise to me, coming of age in my twenties. I thought the goal was to be happy and get as much as I could but that didn't work after a while. It was the people in my life, my connection to them and my usefulness that became the source of sustained rather than fleeting happiness."

Obviously this is just one man's conclusion of what is important and it's up to each of us as we journey through the middle passage to find our own answers or at the very least begin to ask the questions— rather than distract ourselves with drink and drugs or pretend that going to the gym, having plastic surgery, or lying about our age is going to stop the clock.

Promotes living in the moment

If we're not going to live forever, the time we do have left becomes more vital. Returning to the writer Jeanette Winterson, I treasure her advice from another radio interview: "Life is so short and there's only one way to prolong it. Live for what you love. Don't give into indifference." It is more than just opting for what gives your live meaning, but being mindful rather than on autopilot.

Philip Zimbardo is a past president of the American Psychological Association and professor emeritus at Stanford University who has written extensively about time perspectives. He got people to examine how much mental time they spent in the future (planning what to eat for supper, worrying about tomorrow's dental appointment, looking forward to a party at the weekend, or imagining where their career or marriage will be in ten years' time); how much in the past (going over old arguments and sifting through ancient grudges or nostalgia for when the children were small and property prices were low); and how much in the here and now (appreciating the sights, sounds, and smells around them or enjoying the task at hand). He found that people spent a surprisingly small amount of time focused on the present. We are so wrapped up in the past or anxious about the future that we virtually sleepwalk through our lives. Luckily, the crisis of being middle-aged and the realization that we are not going to live forever can focus us back on now and banish indifference.

If you'd like to read more about mindfulness—which is all about being in the present—I have some recommendations at the back of this book.

Opens you up to an alternative view of being elderly

A lot of our fear of aging comes from the fact that we can only imagine what it is like to be elderly from our forty- or fifty-something perspective. From here, being elderly seems defined by loss and decline—but how true is this picture? Sir John Tavener (1944–2013) was a British composer best known for his religious works including "Song for Athene," which was played during the funeral of Diana, Princess of Wales. After a heart attack in 2007, he said: "Suffering is a kind of ecstasy, in a way. Having pain all the time makes me terribly, terribly grateful for every moment I've got."

I have to be honest, I can't get my head around the link between suffering and ecstasy, but then I'm in my late fifties. I doubt my thirty-something self would believe just how exciting I find life now and how full of possibilities. I think he would have been concentrating on the loss of youth (and would have thought that losing all his hair would be the end of life as he knew it!). Being elderly will be more complex than any of us middle-aged people can truly imagine. I feel sure that if we can stare into the darkness, rather than closing our eyes or running away, we will make out shades of gray and chinks of light.

Learning

There is one upside to any experience, however gruesome: you can learn something important.

First, growing old is the preferred alternative to dying young: I never dread another birthday because I feel grateful to be alive. Second, there is a creative tension to life being both limited and limitless. I started writing plays and books after my partner's death; creative people will attest to the importance of limits for inspiration. (I have met writers who, faced with the tyranny of the blank page, write a line of poetry to kickstart a short story; and composers who write in response to the music of the greats.) Third, a fear of death is really an anxiety about not living life to the full now. If we learn how to fully live, we can place death in its true perspective.

APPROACHING SPIRITUALITY

The central tasks of the middle passage—finding your true self and making your life meaningful—prompt bigger questions about what the British writer Douglas Adams (1952–2001) called "life, the universe and everything." Letting go of the idea of the great other and having a realistic relationship with the universe (and giving up the fantasy of being able to control all events) can also make us question whether there is some greater power out there. I'm not going to provide answers but I will try and explain how spirituality can help you through the middle passage.

Jung divided up the journey from cradle to grave into three conflicts:

1. Parents v. Ego

2. Ego v. Self

3. Self v. Infinite.

The ego is the "I want" part of ourselves, our need to get our own way—and damn everybody else. It's the part of us that needs to be admired, respected, and led to the front of the queue (we're back with building towers to our greater glory).

The self is harder to explain but I translate it as "true self" and some therapists call it the "soul." Jung talks of self as the unique individual that each of us is meant to become.

The infinite can be the wider community, our country, the natural world, and the greater universe. It can also be about contemplating how short our time on earth is and thinking about the impact of those who came before us and those who will follow on. It is also about engaging with the deeper mysteries of being human.

In each of these conflicts, it is not about one force winning over the other, but finding a balance. Parents need to socialize their children so they will share nicely with their siblings and friends. In this way, it is not too much of a shock to go to school and not be the center of attention. However, unless children have a healthy ego—and a good sense of themselves—they risk being trampled over by their classmates. Without the drive that our ego provides, it is hard to go out into the world and start a family of your own (because you would always be asking for your parents' permission).

The job of the middle passage is to find a balance between ego and self. We need to know who we are and to find a purposeful life (for our self), but we still need drive and energy to do so (which comes from the ego).

When you can answer "What gives my life meaning?" it is natural to ask "What is the meaning of life?" "Who am I?" becomes "How do I fit into the wider world?" Self v. infinite is about answering these spiritual questions and becoming a full adult.

If you find it helpful to know what's coming up ahead and you're interested in spirituality, I have some suggestions of where to start:

Psychotherapy

The Latin word *psyche* comes from the Greek word *psukhe*, which means soul, and all good therapy has a spiritual dimension. Your counselor or therapist should provide a contemplative space where you can achieve a greater understanding of yourself, the people you love, and how you fit into the wider world. The writings of Jung, one of the founding fathers of psychotherapy, are imbued with spiritual issues and—like all the major world religions—he uses myth and symbolism to make sense of forces greater than us (that cannot be understood by simple observation or psychological studies in the laboratory). So perhaps it is no surprise that therapy engages with questions about what makes life meaningful.

Meditation

Meditation is an important part of Buddhist and Hindu practice and is becoming increasingly popular in Christianity. Some people concentrate on the breath or chant mantras, and others do walking meditations where they focus on the sensation of their heels and then their toes connecting with the ground or the movement of their arms as they swing by their sides.

Not only can meditation offer a deeper self-awareness, but it helps to detach yourself from your thoughts. One of the founders of mindfulness, Jon Kabat-Zinn, says "you are not your thoughts." By this he means, for example, just because you *think* you are a failure it does not make it true and just because you tell yourself a story that, for example, "your father let you down," this does not necessarily make it true (there are probably competing versions of what happened in your family). Mindfulness (a secular version of Buddhism) will also train your mind not to rush ahead all the time to solve problems but will help you to live in and enjoy the moment.

Meditation with a spiritual dimension seeks to provide not just awareness and understanding but wisdom about our essential nature and what it means to be human.

Movement practices

Yoga can be just a physical practice to keep fit and develop a stronger and more flexible body. There is a mental and spiritual element to yoga where you pay attention to your body without identifying so closely with it. To paraphrase Jon Kabat-Zinn, "you are not your body."

Qigong (pronounced *chee-gong*) means cultivating energy or vitality using Taoist principles—a nondeistic faith based on the writings of Lao Tzu (see the further reading list). It involves slow graceful movements coordinated with your breathing to produce and sustain energy and create a meditative inward focus.

Tai chi is similar to qigong. The movements or "forms" are based on martial arts and the natural movements of birds and other animals. Although it is more elaborate than qigong, some practitioners consider tai chi easier because qigong requires more concentration.

Ritualistic dance is another form of spiritual movement practice. One of the most popular today, with classes in most urban centers, is 5Rhythms. It was developed by Gabrielle Roth (1941–2012) in the US and draws on trance dance states, Eastern philosophy, and Gestalt therapy (which focuses on our experiences in the present moment). The five rhythms are flow, staccato, chaos, lyrical, and stillness. The idea is that each dancer interprets the music in their own unique way rather than following choreographed steps. It becomes a form of personal moving meditation, but there are sections where you interact with other members of the class.

Retreat

There are many different kinds of retreat; some follow the principles of specific faiths and others are nondenominational. The idea is to get away from the rat race, personal responsibilities, or a bad emotional situation. With no gossip, no grumbling, no meetings, and no decisions to make, you can go inside yourself or contemplate nature (many centers are in remote and beautiful areas of the country). Some retreats are silent and some provide quiet physical activities like walking, swimming, painting, and special themed events. It can be just a refreshing and relaxing experience—with the opportunity to think differently—or there can be a spiritual dimension.

Organized religions

Finding the right religious practice is a very personal journey. Some people return to the church of their youth, and others had bad experiences and look for different communities to join.

Richard Rohr is a Franciscan monk from New Mexico and the author of many Christian spiritual texts. He draws on Greek myth, Jungian analysis and poetry, and has read widely about other faiths and ancient spiritual practices. In his book *Falling Upward: A spirituality for the two halves of life* (Joessey-Bass, 2011), he warns that most churches are better at catering for the first half of our life (childhood and provisional adulthood) than the second half (when you have been through the middle passage and reached full adulthood). He writes:

"Don't expect or demand from groups what they usually cannot give. Doing so will make you needlessly angry and reactionary. They must and will be concerned with identity, boundaries, self-maintenance, self-perpetuation and self-congratulation. This is their nature and purpose."

Being told what to believe, what to do and what to eat, etc. can provide a useful containing force when we're young, but in the second half of life, the journey is bigger and is about finding our own answers and values (rather than ones handed down off the shelf). Therefore, expect your search for a spiritual home or community to take time.

ANSWERING THE TWO REMAINING KEY QUESTIONS

By this stage, I hope you've begun to grapple with "Who am I." The middle passage poses two more existential questions:

EXERCISE WHAT ARE MY VALUES?

Brainstorming is a good place to start to answer this question. Once you've got all your thoughts down on paper, you can cross out ideas that don't quite ring true and later add others as they occur to you.

This is what Geoffrey wrote:

I believe that everyone is of value

I don't deliberately harm

I do unto others as I'd have them do unto me

I don't let people down

I aim to have enough money to do what I want

I value people above property

I don't need others' approval

My financial affairs are my concern and I choose to share them when it suits me

Relationships: I don't push them to be more than they are or can be

If we continue to talk and listen we can work it out.

WHAT GIVES MY LIFE MEANING?

There is no right or wrong answer. It is up to each of us to find what works for us and my answer will probably not be your answer. To truly own what gives your life meaning, try writing it down. I've left a space below, or write it where you'll see it on a regular basis.

_____

_____

_____

_____

_____

WELL-MADE PLAN

The idea that our life is up to us is daunting, but it's also liberating. Instead of blaming others for letting us down, it's time to roll up our sleeves and make our own lives meaningful. The stakes are high and the potential fallout huge, so how do you know if you're heading in the right direction or if you're about to tip your life from crisis into chaos? First, make a plan. There are four elements to a well-made plan:

1. Time

One of my mantras is *I need to explore and understand before I act.* When you're in pain, the temptation is to rush to act (so as to feel better immediately). If your plan will cause conflict, the temptation is to avoid understanding how it will affect others (for fear of being derailed by their issues). You might have set yourself an arbitrary deadline and started to panic as the date looms (so you act on the spur of the moment rather than thinking the stages of your plan through).

Christopher had first come to see me when he was forty-seven and trying to find a wife and start a family. I was interested in getting him to put dating on hold and understand why he hadn't been able to make a relationship last longer than a couple of months. He kept telling me: "I'm running out of time, I've got to be married by fifty or I'll be too old to be a good father." So I listened to why the current girlfriend wasn't right and supported him through the inevitable crises and helped him review his various strategies for finding a wife, but he was in too much of a hurry to look deeper into the underlying problems. Eventually, we took a break from counseling—to give time for his latest plan to find a wife to bear fruit—but he came back, every so often, to keep me posted on his progress.

A couple of years later, Christopher's mother died and he finally admitted to me: "I'm frightened of relationships. My parents' marriage was miserable and I'm terrified of being trapped in an unloving environment." At this point, he stopped worrying about the ticking clock in his head and started to engage with the work of exploring and understanding himself.

Turn it around: When I asked Christopher how he imagined we would split the time between "exploring" and "understanding" and "action," like many clients he thought it would be a third for each. In fact, you need to spend about 90 percent of the time exploring and understanding because if you get those stages right, the action you need to take almost takes care of itself. So don't rush your plan: it's probably taken many years for you to reach this point in your life, and you don't have to change everything overnight.

2. Balance

If you're really unhappy at the moment and your life seems meaningless and empty, it is probably because you've been following other people's or society's agenda. You may have told yourself "I don't want to upset my partner because he or she will make my life a misery" or "I've got to do what is best for the children" or "If I keep my head down everything will blow over." A person can only take so much downplaying of their needs and emotions before they snap—and probably start an affair. At this point, the rationalizing goes out the window and you start to follow your heart (and ignore your head). Just remember—to make a *wise* decision, you need to follow *both* your head *and* your heart.

When Armando's wife found about his affair, he realized that he would have to end it:

"I come from a very religious family and it would kill my parents if they found out," he said. "I thought of myself on my deathbed and how my children would still not have forgiven me for hurting my wife and I knew I had no choice." Although he stopped sleeping with his mistress, he would regularly phone her "to see how she was coping" and they had been out to dinner on one occasion.

"What impact is this having on everybody?" I asked.

"My girlfriend cries all the time but what can I do?" he said.

"What about your wife?"

"She is angry and suspicious. She thinks the affair is still going on."

"In a sense, it is. You've moved from a full-blown to an emotional affair."

"Can't my girlfriend and I have just have a close friendship?"

Armando was talking entirely from the heart and ignoring his head. How could his girlfriend move on if he was texting her and taking her out? How could his wife trust him if he was seeing the other woman and being economical with the truth about how often he spoke to or saw her? How could he repair his marriage while this "friendship" occupied so much of his emotional energy?

Turn it around: There are three ways of settling disputes. If you're a people-pleaser, you will have opted for the first one: passivity. You treat your needs, wants, and beliefs as if they are of less importance than everybody else's. When you finally have enough of giving and seemingly getting nothing back, you snap and move into the second way of settling a dispute: being domineering. At this point, you elevate your needs, wants, and beliefs as more important than everybody else's.

Lots of couples find a sort of balance by dividing up responsibilities. One partner will be domineering, for example, in the home and over issues to do with the children, and the other may be in charge of money and operate largely in the wider world.

There is another way. Your needs, wants, and beliefs are important, but so are your partner's. I call this third option being assertive. It's best summed up with another one of my mantras: *I can ask, you can say no, and we can negotiate.* Unfortunately, as I've explained, we find it hard to ask (for fear of being turned down) and to say no (in case our partner won't love us any more) and it is hard to negotiate if your parents set you the example of burying their issues or fighting like cat and dog. If you find it hard to be assertive, start with small issues—like what to do this weekend—and build up to larger ones over time.

I will be returning to assertiveness later because it is one of the three skills that I hope you will take away from this book.

3. The big picture

It is important to consider the impact of your plan on other people and across time. Neil, fifty-eight, had left his wife ten years previously for another woman:

"The pain was so great, I just walked out and left a note. At the time, I thought: Why give myself all the grief and upset of being shouted at? So I put a note on the kitchen table along with my keys, and closed the front door behind me, but I never considered the ramifications. Ten years later, I have patched things up with my daughter but she is still angry with me for 'not handling it well.' I was not invited to her wedding as her mother didn't want me to 'spoil the day.' I can't tell you how hard that was and, of course, I don't go to my grandchildren's birthday parties if my ex-wife is going to be there. I wonder now if I could have handled it differently."

Neil had since remarried (not to the woman he left his wife for) but he never expected the fallout to last for so long.

"I would still have left," he said, "but if I could have had my time over, I would have faced my wife and explained everything to my daughter rather than leaving a note."

Turn it around: I am not saying that you have to stick with a marriage that is not working just to keep other people happy, because that's not the recipe for a meaningful life. However, if you spend time trying to work through the issues and talking about what is making you unhappy, it is possible to reach a mutual decision: Where you decide together to end the marriage rather than one of you imposing the decision on the other.

When Ian and Sally, in their late forties with two preteen children, arrived in counseling, their aims were diametrically opposed. She felt they were "too different" and wanted to end the marriage, and he wanted to try again. So I suggested working on their communication, which could be useful whatever the outcome. It could lay the foundation for a better relationship or if they went on to separate it would help them to cooperate as co-parents. After about six weeks, it became clear that Sally was adamant and they began to discuss a temporary separation. When we had finished our work together, Ian had a new confession to make: "I didn't realize just how unhappy I'd been in the marriage. I was so preoccupied with talking up everything, I didn't face up to the deeper problems." The decision to get divorced had become a mutual one.

4. Test it out

When you're making a big decision, it is always a good idea to talk through the plan with someone whose opinions you respect. Martin, fifty-nine, came to me with his wife Margaret, fifty-seven, for help recovering from the affair he'd had with a much younger woman while he was working abroad.

"I spent a lot of money on her that I didn't really have—five-star hotels, luxury presents, little vacations, you know the sort of thing," he explained.

"As if that was the only problem," Margaret cut in.

"I was taken for a fool, I was flattered by the attention. It made me feel young to be in her company."

"Trying to dig himself out of a hole, he's emptied out our pension fund, our future. There is nothing left." Margaret's despair was written across her face.

Martin had made a fortune in his thirties in mining and quarrying by building up a portfolio of sites across the world and prospecting on them. In most cases, there was no profit or a loss, but some of them had paid off in the most spectacular way.

"So I did the same again but perhaps my touch has left me ..." His voice trailed away.

"Our son—who works in the same industry—tried to warn you. It was madness but would you listen?"

"It worked before," he said.

Martin had failed to realize that we have different needs approaching sixty (when security is important) from starting out in our thirties (when there's plenty of time to recover from financial mistakes). If he had consulted more widely—rather than imagining he was responding to his gut feelings but more likely his panic and shame—it is unlikely he would have made the same investments.

Turn it around: It can seem like we need big changes to solve big problems (and feeling that your life doesn't make sense any more fits into that category!), but it is better to break everything down into small steps, review constantly, and adjust accordingly. Over time, you will reach the goal of radical change. (You might discover that your life is basically OK but you need to make small changes to make it more meaningful.)

BECOME YOUR OWN PHILOSOPHER

Instead of thinking the answers are all out there—very much a first half of life idea—I'd like you to consider that the truth might be within. The great advantage of being forty- or fifty-something is that you have accumulated enough experience and wisdom to become your own philosopher. So how do you start on this journey?

EXERCISE | LOOK INSIDE

Understand your influences by asking the following questions:

1. What were my mother's beliefs when I was growing up?

2. What were my father's beliefs when I was growing up?

3. What did my school believe?

4. What did I believe in my twenties?

5. What did I believe in my thirties?

6. What does my employer/company believe?

7. What does contemporary society believe?

Try to place these historic influences on you into one core belief. It helps if you can condense it into one sentence. For example, I find many people have some variation on this belief: "I must do everything perfectly and satisfy everybody or I have totally failed."

Challenge your beliefs

Write your core beliefs down and ask yourself the following questions:

1. What are the positives of this belief?

2. What are the downsides of this belief?

3. What's been the impact of this belief on my life to date?

4. How useful is this belief for the second half of my life?

5. What would I like to change about this belief.

Fresh perspectives

When you are putting together your plans for the future or feeling overwhelmed by the road ahead, ask yourself the following questions:

1. What evidence do I have that this thought is true?

2. How else could I view my situation?

3. What is the worst that could happen and what would it mean to my life?

4. Even if the depressing, anxious, or overwhelming thoughts are realistic, what can I do to improve the situation?

COMMUNICATING WITH YOUR PARTNER

When your life has stopped making sense, your energy is more focused on trying to find a way forward than considering the impact on those closest to you. As you are reading this book, my guess is that relations between you and your partner have become difficult, strained, and even toxic. Even if you have generally good communication, he or she may be anxious about the future and more likely to shut down or jump to the wrong conclusions.

My aim is to help you work as a team to find a new way of living that will be meaningful for you both. But before your partner is ready to listen to your plans for the future, it might be necessary to listen to him or her. So follow these six stages:

Step into your partner's shoes

Think back to when you became unhappy and imagine that you're watching a movie that covers all the events and your behavior from that moment to today. What are the key moments? What bits are most distressing to watch? Now imagine watching the movie again but from your partner's perspective: What would that be like?

Think about what have you said during this period. What must it have been like to be on the receiving end of your comments—even if you've apologized or have taken back the criticism or blame? How much of what's been happening recently have you tried to explain to your partner? Or has he or she been in the dark and unsure?

Your struggle with the middle passage has probably been difficult for your partner too and he or she may be anxious, confused, and possibly also depressed. What you hear as anger could simply be distress.

Acknowledge your partner's feelings

Good communication is not just sharing what it is like to be you, but finding out what it is like to be your partner. So the next time you see that your partner is upset, try and pinpoint what the feeling might be. For example, "I can see that you're sad." Don't worry if you get the feeling wrong, because your partner will be happy to clarify. I know it is tempting to switch off or walk away when faced with a barrage of emotions and you certainly don't want to invite an out-pouring of grief. But if you acknowledge your partner's anger (or whatever they are feeling) and show a real interest in understanding the causes, it may soon burn off and you can have a reasonable dis-cussion. Trying to shut down your partner's feelings, rationalize them away, or ignore them will make him or her more upset and more likely to explode.

Make a fulsome apology

Once you have reviewed your behavior and gained a greater understanding of the impact on your partner, I hope there is some-thing that you regret. Instead of keeping it to yourself, I would like you to make a fulsome apology.

Let me explain. Most apologies are undermined by an explana-tion about why we behaved in a particular way. Explanations can then be interpreted as making excuses and undermine the power of the apology. So start with a fulsome apology, for example: "I locked myself away and didn't communicate the depth of my distress to you." Next identify the impact on your partner: "You must have felt excluded, anxious, and disrespected." Finally, make a commitment to change. For example, "I am going to make an effort to talk on a regular basis and if you ask 'What's the matter' I will not reply 'Nothing.'"

At this point, it is important to listen rather than talk more—which can easily slip into explaining and excuses. Your partner might not respond at all to your apology—he or she might be handling lots of conflicting emotions. However, it will change the atmosphere in your relationship and help facilitate the next few steps. (There is more information about fulsome apologies in the next chapter.)

Acknowledge the good things in your relationship

It's OK for me to think it is normal and healthy to question everything in your forties and fifties—and that includes your relationship. From your partner's perspective, this will seem like constant criticism of him or her and an attempt to destroy everything you've built together.

Time and time again, I see couples where one partner is questioning everything (and finding little or nothing of value in their marriage) and the other one is defending (and building the marriage into an almost sacred union of two souls destined to be together). Does this sound familiar? The more you focus on the negatives in order to make yourself heard, like pushing down on a seesaw, the more your partner will soar into the air with reasons to stay together. No wonder your relationship is such a bumpy ride. So how do you calm things down? Just like on a seesaw, by coming into the middle.

If you tell your partner what you appreciate about your relationship (even if it is about the past) and the qualities that you admire about him or her (so you don't come across as so critical), it will help open up a more fruitful dialogue. With you acknowledging the good things in your marriage, your partner can finally acknowledge what hasn't been working for him or her too. If you are less critical of your partner, he or she will be less critical of you. With a virtuous circle, rather than a negative one, you can start communicating effectively—rather than simply blaming each other.

Negotiate

In order to improve communication, I have asked you to step into your partner's shoes, acknowledge his or her feelings, make a fulsome apology, and acknowledge the good things in your relationship. It comes as a surprise to most people that there are four previous steps before arriving at what they imagine should be the first: Laying the proposals on the table. Even though we've reached negotiation, I would rather you *still* held back. If you present a plan for the future, your partner may say no. If instead you involve him or her in the process, you not only double the brain power but he or she is more likely to buy into something that you have created together.

Start with discussing what you both agree on (like "we want the best for the children") and reminding each other of the positives (for example, overcoming past problems together). Now you are ready to look at the issues between you. Listen carefully to your partner's proposals—even if they seem a backward step—and ask questions so you can double-check you've heard correctly or to flesh out details. If you give your partner a respectful hearing, he or she should reciprocate and listen to your proposed plan.

Stay in the ring of pain

You're not going to like the last step. Instead of rushing to make things better, or trying to rationalize away or discount your partner's concerns, I'd like you to say to your partner: "Tell me more." I know it is tough but I think you're old and wise enough now to cope, so take a couple of deep breaths. It will not be pleasant but it is better to listen than running away or sweeping everything under the carpet. When it is your turn to respond, try to keep calm so your voice is neutral and your body language is open-hearted.

The good news is that each time you stay in the ring of pain, it gets a little easier and your discussions will become more fruitful. Ultimately, you can become a team to build a new life together or you can separate with the least harm done to each other and your children. There is no rush to make a decision and you will learn a lot about yourself, your partner, relationships, and life in the process.

CONCLUSION

Being forty- or fifty-something is a great time to dig deeper (to understand yourself better or recover important parts of your character abandoned earlier in the journey but still needed), to expand your repertoire (because what worked in part one is not necessarily right for part two), and to stop going through the motions (as time is too precious to live on autopilot). Also, becoming a full-adult—as opposed to a teenager in adult clothes—involves acknowledging that your choices impact on other people. It doesn't mean that you have to lead your life according to their strictures, but you do need to be compassionate, and find a formula that will satisfy you and your partner.

I have asked your partner to read the first half of the book (because I think he or she will learn something important about his or her own journey through the middle passage) and I'd like to invite you to read the second half too. It will not only give you an insight into your partner's viewpoint but I will go into greater depth about Adult to Adult Communication (Transactional Analysis) and Assertiveness—two of the most important skills for transforming your life. I will also introduce a concept that will change how you approach disputes—which you need to be forty- or fifty-something to understand.

SUMMING UP

➤ Being forty- or fifty-something is a great time to meet your true self and finally become your own person.

➤ Although it is unsettling to contemplate your mortality, being conscious that time is limited will help you live more meaningfully.

➤ To work as a team to find a way forward, spend as much time really listening to your partner as you do trying to convince him or her to agree to your plans.

PART TWO

My partner is having a midlife crisis

CHAPTER SIX

How to stay sane in an insane situation

You thought you had a good relationship, not perfect because nothing is, but you had fun together. The children were doing fine and although you've had your fair share of problems, the two of you were chugging along. However, somehow, your husband or wife seemed to become dissatisfied with everything or wanted to run away from his or her responsibilities, started drinking more, and became generally short-tempered. At first, you didn't really notice, or put it down to work worries or not sleeping well or issues with one of your children. And then your partner started looking up old friends on Facebook, launched a keep fit campaign, or found a new circle of friends (but excluded you). It all happened so gradually that you can't really put your finger on when your husband or wife turned into a stranger, or perhaps you can date it to the time you found an incriminating text from a work colleague or one of those new friends.

Whatever the background, things have gone from bad to worse and your husband or wife is becoming difficult, moody, and sometimes downright spiteful. He or she rarely wants to spend time with you and when you try to talk about what has been going on, you have been fobbed off, attacked, or blamed for all of your partner's problems. No wonder you're confused, angry, and feeling at the end of your tether.

So what has it been like reading the first part of the book? (If you haven't read it yet, please do so as I will be referring back to concepts and ideas that I've already introduced and it is important to properly understand your partner's viewpoint before trying to repair your marriage.) I hope it has been helpful to have an insight into the darker corner of your partner's mind and the task ahead does not seem too overwhelming. However, I wouldn't be surprised if my compassion for your partner has got your back up: "Doesn't he realize the pain he is causing?" Alternatively, you've been going, "Yes, but …" and wonder if I understand the depth of your shock, pain, and betrayal.

I've counseled hundreds of people on the receiving end of this kind of behavior and I know the devastation it can cause. I've also worked with adults whose parents split up when they were young, so I know how high the stakes can be. However, I need to explain why "Yes but" might be a natural response (and a very understandable one too), but there is a better one which will help you and your partner work as a team together. My job is to see all sides and build bridges. I believe that you can come through this crisis and feel stronger, wiser, and happier and—equally important—protect your children from the worst of the fallout.

EXERCISE IMPROVE YOUR SLEEP PATTERNS

Everything seems worse after a bad night's sleep. If you're anxious and your mind is racing, try the sound and thought meditation exercise from chapter three and the progressive relaxation exercise from chapter four. If you are feeling depressed—which often leads to early-morning wakening—this exercise will be particularly helpful. Improving your sleep patterns will help you cope better.

1. *Have a regular bed and wake-up time.* As much as possible, go to bed at the same time rather than waiting until you are sleepy. It will help to reset your body clock. If you find it hard to drop off, do the progressive relaxation or a simple breath meditation (where you

focus on the air going in and out of your nostrils and gently push thoughts to one side).

2. *Invest in good sleep.* The recommendation is to change your mattress every eight years and the pillow every two years.

3. *Get out of bed if you can't sleep after half an hour.* Your bedroom is your sleeping place, not your lying awake place. So go into another room and jot down the intrusive thoughts on a piece of paper or do a jigsaw or some activity that only partly engages your brain.

4. *Don't worry about wakefulness.* It is natural to wake from time to time. If you don't worry about waking up, you are more likely to fall asleep again—and nighttime worrying rarely solves a problem.

5. *If you wake up, be mindful.* You are most likely to slip through a moment of wakefulness by being mindful, rather than tossing and turning. Focus on how your body connects with the mattress, which will help push away anxious thoughts.

6. *Don't work, read, or watch TV in the bedroom.* I would also leave your phone out of the bedroom so it is not flashing or bleeping during the night and you're not checking your messages (when you should be preparing for sleep). Remember, your bedroom is for un-winding rather than stimulating your mind.

7. *Have fixed eating times.* This will also help to regulate your body clock.

8. *Cut out alcohol.* Although, at the start, alcohol is a sedative, regular drinking will keep you awake at night.

9. *No caffeine after breakfast.* I find this one impossible to follow and if you have similar concerns make it a later time, like 11 a.m. or lunchtime. Caffeine includes tea, cola, energy drinks, and chocolate. If you are a smoker remember that cigarettes are stimulants too, so try and find a similar cutoff point earlier in the day.

10. *Try late-afternoon exercise.* A twenty-minute workout will raise your body temperature, which will then begin to fall in the evening. Falling body temperature is thought to be a trigger for sleep.

FIVE MOST UNHELPFUL REACTIONS TO THE MIDDLE PASSAGE

The middle passage is the time of our lives—normally in our forties and fifties—when we take stock of the first half of our lives, learn from our experiences, and search for a formula for a meaningful and satisfying second half. For lots of people, it is a time of regret, frustration, and upheaval. They start criticizing everything and can act strangely or badly. As you probably know, it is hard being on the receiving end of such behavior. If you don't understand what's behind this abrupt change, you are likely to panic, lash out, or retreat. Don't worry if you're reacting in one or more of the ways described below. These are natural responses to feeling cornered but, unfortunately, they make matters worse:

1. Ignoring it

Every relationship goes through blips and tough times, but you were so busy with day-to-day life and made so many excuses for your partner's behavior that you failed to notice the bad patches were stretching into months and maybe even years.

Sandra, forty-eight, came into counseling after discovering her husband's five-year affair and the huge debts he had run up—on various credit cards—subsidizing his mistress. "My father did the majority of the childcare so we could both work long hours and he would stay on into the evening so it didn't feel so lonely when my husband was working late. A couple of years ago, my father said to me 'Don't you think he's having an affair?' and I laughed at the idea. 'Not my Patrick, he adores me. Everybody says it.' I should have listened. My father wouldn't have said anything unless he had real concerns. If I had heeded his warning, we wouldn't be in such a deep financial hole now."

Turn it around: Although it is good to give your partner the benefit of the doubt sometimes, it is important to listen to your feelings too.

One of my central mantras for helping people to lead a balanced life is: *What is this feeling trying to tell me?* If you keep feeling anxious, there might be a good reason.

2. Accepting the projection

When we have uncomfortable feelings—like anger, disappointment, and regret—we try and ignore them by first denying and then burying them (in what Jung called our shadow side). We can further distance ourselves from these forbidden feelings by, for example, spotting anger in someone else (and overreacting to it). We can also avoid looking at our responsibility, for example, for our own disappointment and regret in our forties and fifties, by blaming someone else (and temporarily feeling better). This behavior is called projection. I often find the partners of people in crisis in their forties and fifties have accepted their partner's projection or partially accepted it (and then got incredibly angry because deep down they believe it's true). The best way to explain this is to give an example.

Maggie had a difficult childhood. Her father had high standards and favored his sons over his daughter, and she was given the message that she had to be perfect. Everything was fine between Maggie and her husband Robin but when they had children, relatively late in life, the problems from the past came back to haunt her:

"I thought everything had to be just so in order for our children to get the best start in life—and when it didn't turn out that way I'd get angry with myself or my husband or the children—sometimes all three—and start shouting." In the meantime, Maggie and Robin had not resumed their sex life after their youngest child was born. "I had postnatal depression but wouldn't admit it and get help. I had pneumonia but wouldn't stop until I was hospitalized. Being an older mom was exhausting and sex slipped so far down my priorities that I didn't really miss it at all." So when she discovered her husband's seven-year affair and he said: "What do you expect if you're angry all the time and withholding sex?" she took on *all* the blame for the affair. "What was I thinking?" she wailed in my counseling room.

Turn it around: I don't like the concept of blame. A lot of the problems of Maggie's marriage could be laid at the door of her perfectionism, but that started in her childhood. Of course, we could blame her father. However, he was a product of a time when people did value sons more than daughters. He drove his children to work hard because he had arrived in this country as a penniless refugee and had known real starvation and deprivation. So should we blame the government in his home country for the war that drove him to leave, or perhaps the insurgents?

In counseling, I encouraged Maggie not to accept her husband's projections surrounding the affair. Could he have explained that the lack of sex was making him miserable?

"He says he did try," she replied. "But it was so subtle that I didn't notice."

In most relationships, the problems are six of one and half a dozen of the other. Just because your partner points the finger—and projects—does not make it right. What would happen if instead of getting angry at the accusations—and giving him or her further ammunition that the marriage is fatally flawed—you tried something else. For example, you could "let it go," ask a question like "What do you mean" or simply laugh. It might make your partner look at his or her own responsibility for how his or her life turned out.

3. Being the critical parent

There are three ideas at the heart of my plan for transforming your marriage into either the loving connected union you've always dreamed of, or helping you to part on reasonably amicable terms. The first idea comes from Transactional Analysis (TA) introduced in part one.

According to TA, we have three parts to our personality: parent, adult, and child. We need them all. Child is the source of our intuition, creativity, and play (which helps us unwind, connect, and facilitate sex). We sometimes need to parent our partner and look after him or her when ill or going through a tough patch. The problem when we repeatedly parent (by which I mean organizing or trying to control) is that our partner will repeatedly respond like a child. Parent is divided into two parts: nurturing and critical. Child is also divided into two parts: free (the positive part I've described above) and adapted (which includes rebelling, switching off, acting defensive, passive-aggressive behavior). Although there is a small place in any

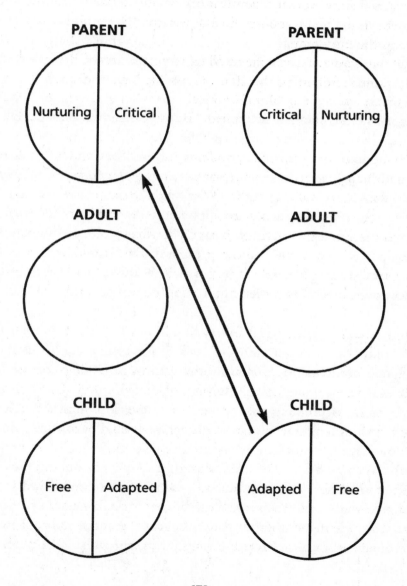

relationship for a bit of critical parenting (because some behavior is unacceptable) and for a bit of adapted child (because these behaviors can be understandable), I see many couples stuck in a fatal combination for most of their time together.

If you behave like a critical parent, your partner will automatically respond as an adapted child. Worse still, his or her adapted child can easily tip over into being critical parent mode and that will send you into adapted child yourself. Although each partner will have a role that they are most comfortable playing, I like to think of it as a tennis match with you taking it in turns to serve and return critical parent and adapted child in a game that goes on for years and years.

Robert, forty-two, felt criticized by his wife all the time. "Everything has to be planned and researched to get the best possible experience for our daughter—to avoid the latest disease and to buy the right organic sock. It's like some multilayered complex project. If I try and help to get our daughter ready, my wife will say 'You'll only get it wrong, so leave it to me.' I don't think I'm useless, but I am by the current standards which are high and unknowable." So while his wife is being a critical parent, he is acting like an adapted child—by being passive-aggressive—and starting an affair. "My wife and I only have sex every eighteen months—which feels like the tolling of the executioner's bell, and I need human contact."

Turn it around: Although it is very tempting to criticize your partner and point out his or her failings, it will prompt sulking, self-justification, or more rebellion. The answer is to move into adult because this will help to promote some adult behavior from your partner. The adult mode is problem-solving and asks questions that start: who, what, why, when, how? For example, Robert could have asked: "How can we solve the problem of our sex life being infrequent?" Alternatively, he could have asked: "What could I do to help you feel more in the mood for sex?" He could have given his view of childhood: That kids are resilient and their needs can be met by family activities rather than them being constantly centerstage or seen as a problem to micromanage (which Robert believed was his wife's vision). Both views are equally valid but couldn't be discussed unless Robert was prepared to express his opinions in a calm way (which is adult) rather than making sarcastic comments (passive aggressive) or withdrawing and hiding his feelings (people-pleasing) to avoid his wife's irritation (which are adapted child behaviors).

4. Becoming the nurturing parent

Your partner is going through a tough time. He or she is depressed, has lost a job, or appears to finds life meaningless. So isn't it natural to be sympathetic and try to help?

Although this trap is much better than critical parent, there is a huge problem with being nurturing parent. You are still trying to manage your partner and, in the nicest way possible, run his or her life. The telltale signs that you're using the nurturing parent mode is that you feel like you're treading on eggshells and your partner keeps accusing you of being patronizing.

Maggie was determined to change and win a second chance for her marriage—even though her husband could not give up the other woman. When her husband wanted time away from both Maggie and his mistress, she found him temporary bed and breakfasts. When he asked her what she wanted for her birthday, she asked him to meditate everyday (because she had found it helpful herself). She phoned his parents to organize weekends away for her husband with them too. Of course, it was better than shouting at him. However, nurturing parent is still part of parent mode and it is easy to slip across to critical parent—especially when Maggie's husband did not appreciate her efforts.

Turn it around: It is difficult enough to run our own lives and know what is best for ourselves and almost impossible to do it for somebody else. In counseling, Maggie started to examine her behavior and discovered it wasn't quite so altruistic. "Yes, I wanted him to have peace from the meditation and space alone and time with his mother—who is showing the early signs of dementia—but I hoped they would all help him come back to me. His mother will remind him of the importance of family. He will miss me and the children when he's alone—rather than with *her*. With a more peaceful mind, could he think straight and make the right choice?"

By being controlling, in the nicest possible way, she was encouraging her husband to go into adapted child and sulk, throw tantrums, and rebel.

Instead Maggie needed to move into adult and by doing so encourage her husband to switch to adult, too. In this way, she could listen to his issues and he could hear her distress (rather than getting defensive). At this point, they could make a plan together for how to move forward—rather than Maggie trying to impose one.

5. Involving the children

If a crisis has been going on for a while, your children will be aware of your distress and your partner's altered behavior. It is only natural that they will ask questions and may offer support—so far so good. Unfortunately, they are likely to take sides.

Alan, fifty-one, and his wife Hannah, forty-five, had two children: a girl of fourteen and a boy of twelve. Alan had an all-engrossing job in the City and Hannah was principally involved with raising the children and running the home (although she did have a part-time job that she fitted in around the children). "I fill my days," said Hannah defensively. "I play a lot of tennis and see my friends and the children still need me. Although it's mostly being ferried here and there." She did not make her life sound particularly fulfilling. She had several unresolved issues from her childhood—her father had left her mother for another woman—but she did not want to address those. There was another topic off limits in counseling, too. Hannah had had a passionate "friendship" with another man (who had recently left his wife) and in Alan's eyes wanted far more from his wife than going off for a cup of coffee together. Alan had also found a series of compromising texts on Hannah's phone.

Although I tried to help Hannah and Alan communicate better, she decided after two sessions that counseling was not for her. However, Alan had a couple of sessions with me—to reduce his anxiety about the future making things worse at home—and reported back on the family's progress from time to time.

"My daughter has been wonderful and offered a female perspective," Alan explained at one of our sessions.

"How is her relationship with her mother?" I asked.

"It's been tense—Hannah accused me of turning our daughter against her when she didn't want to go to the tennis club with Hannah."

Turn it around: The situation between you and your partner is complex and multilayered. It is extremely hard, even for an adult, to understand all the competing versions of how you reached this challenging place. What hope does a child have? Even if your children are now grownup, to properly explain everything you will fall into the "too much information" trap, and it is not fair to draw them into your camp—remember they love both of you! So thank your children for their concern but reassure them that you are dealing with the situation (and speak instead to one of your parents, friends, or a professional). If they have any questions about your partner's behavior, suggest they talk to him or her directly (you're probably the last person that your husband or wife is going to update about his or her feelings). *Never criticize your partner to your children,* keep the information you share with them to the bare minimum and don't comment on the situation (because your children can draw their own conclusions). Finally, don't ask them to be a go-between or to report back on your partner.

FIVE MOST HELPFUL REACTIONS TO THE MIDDLE PASSAGE

I know that at this point everything seems bleak. You've made all these mistakes and a critical voice in your head has started up that's making you feel even worse. However, I wouldn't be at all surprised if—as well as using some of the unhelpful strategies for dealing with the middle passage—you've already started to experiment with some of the helpful ones.

1. Understanding

By getting this far in the book, I hope you've made a giant step forward in understanding what's behind this crisis at home. Your partner might be acting like a stranger, but now you realize that every assumption that he or she has based his or her life on is collapsing, and that his or her world view is crumbling away, the wild and unpredictable behavior will seem less mysterious. I hope that it will also seem less directed at you in particular. The fault lines that the middle passage has exposed were probably there years before you came onto the scene (although your recent reactions could have widened them).

The other important message that I would like you to take away is that everybody has to journey through the middle passage to become a full adult. So take the focus away from your partner and think about what you've learned about yourself and life in general from coping with the fallout.

Sandra, who we met earlier in this chapter, told me:

"I'd lived a rather blessed life until my husband's infidelity and the subsequent financial problems. I had a good job, three great children, supportive parents, a wide circle of friends, and a good standard of living, but I was rather naive and took a lot for granted. I could sympathize when friends had a problem, or with my mother, who had a very disrupted childhood, but I never really understood the depth of their pain until I was hollowed out myself. I feel that I've become a better daughter and friend and I've discovered a whole new level of love for my children (because I know it would break their hearts if I'd taken the easier option and thrown my husband out)."

In a nutshell, Sandra had learned one of the truths that every full adult knows: life is difficult. (While our consumer society tells us that life *should* be easy—as long as we have downloaded this app or bought this wonderful gadget.) There is an upside to knowing this uncomfortable truth: when things don't go the way we planned, we are less likely to blame ourselves and more likely to be compassionate —after all, life is difficult.

Sandra concluded: "I certainly feel that I've been flung into the middle passage myself by my husband's behavior and although I wouldn't have chosen it—not in a million, trillion years—it hasn't been all bad."

2. Listening calmly with a curious mind

When your partner is critical of you, it is natural to defend yourself, get upset, or fight back. These reactions do nothing to resolve the underlying problems and can lead to a cycle of bruising rows that can make your partner feel there is no hope (or they may use the rows as evidence that splitting up is inevitable). There is one simple thing you can do that could revolutionize your relationship: listen with a curious mind.

I had been working with Judith and Anton—both in their late fifties with three children—since Anton announced that he couldn't stand living with Judith any more and rented an apartment nearby (so he could visit their two younger children who were still living at home). I soon discovered the pattern at the heart of their problems. Anton was a people-pleaser and if Judith got upset he would cave in and do anything to appease her. Over an eighteen-month period, we worked on their relationship. First, we focused on small things—like disagreements over who should sit next to who at a family theater outing—and then we moved onto larger issues—like resuming their sex life. We took some breaks when Anton was not yet ready to move back into the family home, and we had a final session after they had bought a new home together (and were enjoying the project of furnishing it together). As part of the exit from counseling, I always ask couples what they have learned about themselves and what turned round their relationship.

"I felt that I was being listened to," Anton explained, "and it wasn't the end of the world if I disagreed."

"Before counseling, I had very fixed views about what was right or wrong—particularly about bringing up the children," said Judith. "What I've learned is that Anton might have a different opinion but that's all right because two heads are generally better than one."

"I've also learned to be braver. My opinions are equally valid and I'm not afraid to stand my ground any more," said Anton.

To reach this virtuous circle—where one partner's positive behavior encouraged more positive behavior from the other—it was necessary for Judith to listen. When she felt upset by what she heard—which happened a lot in the early days because Anton needed to get a lot off his chest—she took a couple of deep breaths. By remaining calm, she could access her curious mind and ask a question (for example: How often did this happen?) or a clarification (for example: Could you give me an example of when you felt like that?).

3. Take a step back

I have talked about the negative side of projection—where someone distances themselves from a part of their personality they dislike by first disowning it and then casting it onto someone else (and criticizing them). There is a more benign side to projection—often called positive projection. Have you ever watched two people click on a first date? Of course, it's partly sexual chemistry but it's also projection. They have all these fantasies of what would make the perfect partner and project them onto the blank sheet of the stranger opposite them. I had one couple where she thought he was strong (but actually he was just suppressing all his emotions), and he thought she was warm and open (but missed that she was incredibly anxious and was spilling unprocessed feelings all over the place). The biggest surprise for some of my couples is that they didn't marry themselves! By which I mean they were convinced that their partner felt the same way they did: that they were fundamentally the same person (but wearing different clothes) and therefore would act like they expected them to and agree to all their wishes (or should that be demands?).

I know there is a lot of projection going on when a client uses the word "should" a lot. For example, I appeared on a TV debate about how to childproof marriage. My position was that people get married because they enjoy spending time together but, after children, it is easy for the only meaningful interaction to be exchanging lists of instructions about their care. The person debating the opposite view was a romantic novelist who proudly told me that she always put her four children first and now her grandchildren. When I questioned how her husband might feel about that, she told me: "He loves me enough to understand," and: "Men *should* understand how important children are to their wives."

"And they *should* provide for their family without any complaint—even if it comes at a great cost to themselves?" I asked, and she nodded. "And they *should* do everything their wife asks?"

She almost nodded again but realized that I was teasing her and laughed.

Perhaps I shouldn't have been surprised that a romantic novelist believed the fundamental premise for all fairy-tales: someday my prince or princess will come and I'll get everything I want.

Positive projection can bind two people together and help us overcome our fear of hitching our life up to a complete stranger, but we are projecting some of our own strengths and inner resources onto our partner, too. By the time we reach our forties and fifties, we should be able to take care of our own emotional needs (rather than outsource to our partner) and, assuming our children are past the baby stage, provide for our own physical needs (rather than be completely financially reliant on our partner). In other words, we can sort out our own lives—thank you.

So by taking a step back and understanding how positive projection works you should have a more realistic view of your partner (as "crooked timber"—see chapter four) rather than setting him or her up as the source of all your happiness. If you've been able to do that, there will be two important changes.

First, the temperature of your discussions is likely to go down. You can start to listen to what your partner is actually saying (rather than jumping to the worst conclusions), so the chance of reaching a compromise (suitable to both parties) increases. Second, you will become more aware of your own strengths and abilities.

You may love your partner dearly—and that's a great asset at a difficult time—but if he or she left tomorrow, your life would not be robbed of all meaning.

4. Introduce a new way of thinking

I don't introduce this next idea until my clients are going through the middle passage, because they need enough experience of the world and sufficient maturity to understand it.

So what is the idea?

There are two ways of thinking. The first is called Comparative Thinking, which is what we generally use in the first half of our lives. The second is referred to as Contemplative Thinking and it is what we need in the second half of our life and to reach full adulthood. Let's start with comparative thinking because you'll be only too familiar with it.

We are frequently being asked to compare two different items and decide which is better—which washing powder washes whiter, whether margarine is better than butter, whether we want coffee or tea, red or white wine, brown or white bread, chicken or fish. On TV talent shows, there are often two contestants who receive the least votes and have to compete again for the judges. In politics, will our elected representative vote for or against a piece of legislation and—in a referendum—are you for or against the proposal? The implication is always that one choice must be better than the other.

However, comparative thinking goes deeper than which of two items we prefer. We tend to divide everything into one camp or the other. I remember being confused about the war in the Balkans in the nineties: who were the goodies and who were the baddies? Behavior is right or wrong. People are winners or losers. A date is either a success or a failure. If you found my compassion for your partner, in the first half of the book, difficult to stomach and you kept on going, "Yes, but," it is probably because you were using comparative thinking. If I was saying his or her behavior was understandable and even necessary, it could have been read as he or she was "right". Guess what that would have made you? "Wrong." No wonder, you were angry and wanted to take exception to everything I was saying.

While comparative thinking is either/or, contemplative thinking embraces both viewpoints. Instead of "Yes, but …" it is "Yes, and … ". In a nutshell, your partner has a valid position (he or she must follow a path that makes him or her happy) and your position is equally valid too (of course he or she has to be aware of the impact on other people and take that into consideration too). You're *both* right! I know you're going to have lots of questions about how to settle arguments if you're both right. Don't worry. It is natural to have misgivings. Comparative thinking is so deeply ingrained in us that it takes a while to get your head around contemplative thinking. Therefore, in this chapter, I will explore what contemplative thinking means and in chapter eight explain how it can provide a breakthrough for your relationship.

Comparative Thinking	Contemplative Thinking
Yes, but …	Yes, and …
Either/or	Both
Narrow	Expansive
Exposing differences	Uncovering similarities
All or nothing	Inclusive
Labeling	Beyond labels
Differences	Similarities
Combative	Collaborative

So let's look at comparative and contemplative thinking in action.

We met Jacob and Molly in chapter five. He had gone to a massage parlor and we were working on repairing their marriage (and also helping them both deal with the fallout from Jacob taking early retirement). Restarting their sex life was fraught—not only because of the hurt caused by his infidelity, but also because they had longstanding issues about frequency and different ideas of what they wanted from lovemaking. For Jacob, if the choice was between sex with ejaculation and a simple cuddle, he would always take the first option.

"Surely, it's got to be better?" he asked me.

"What about sex with Molly having an orgasm or sex with her enjoying herself but not climaxing?"

"I'm a generous man. It's got to be giving her an orgasm, too," he replied confidently.

"But that puts me under huge pressure. There's times when I don't necessarily want one or when I don't climax, then I'm a failure," Molly told him.

I tried to take the heat out of the discussion by comparing our choices in the bedroom to choices in a restaurant: "Sometimes you want a steak supper but there are other times when a bowl of soup hits the mark," I suggested.

"That one's easy, steak supper every time," he said. "I get a bit obsessional and I'll have one favorite meal which I'll have over and over again until I get fed up and switch onto something else being the best."

When I looked into what was stopping Molly from being intimate with Jacob, I realized she was doing plenty of comparative thinking, too.

"He will be comparing me with the masseuse, younger versus older. Size 16 versus size 10. Novelty versus familiar. Isn't it obvious why I don't want to put myself through all that?"

To break the deadlock, I highlighted their dilemma using contemplative thinking.

"Nobody in a loving relationship should be made to have sex they don't want [Molly's position] *and* nobody should have to do without the sex they do want [Jacob's position]. Both of your positions are equally valid."

At this point, the tension between them disappeared and we could start to discuss how they might gradually reintroduce physical intimacy in a way that suited them both. (For more about this idea, see my previous book *Have the Sex You Want: A couple's guide for getting back the spark.*)

Another example of comparative thinking is James and Patty from chapter one. James had had an affair with a younger woman while he was working abroad. Although it had finished over a year previously, James had kept in touch with the woman for several months as "friends." Patty's confidence was undermined because although James seemed committed to working on their marriage, he also said he needed space and lived in an apartment on his own. In the previous two weeks, James had returned to the country where the affair had taken place for another work project.

"I had to give seminars from morning to night," he said. "I also contacted Patty several times a day—FaceTime too, so she could see I was in my work cubicle rather that out on the town."

James had worked around the clock and arrived in my office straight from the airport, not having slept for eighteen hours. He now had two choices: unwinding alone on a beach for a couple of days or working on his marriage.

"The old James would have worked on his marriage," said Patty.

"But the old James was an illusion," explained James. "I tried to make everybody happy and ended up empty and resentful."

"I get that but I don't know the new James," Patty replied.

Once again, we were in comparative thinking with the old James = good and new James = bad. I could see lots of things that weren't working for the old James (so I would question whether this was good for him or even Patty). Meanwhile, the new James was learning to say no and accepting that making Patty happy was not his job (after all, she was responsible for her own happiness). It might have been uncomfortable, for both of them, but it was certainly not all "bad."

Fortunately, they were committed to learning and growing and were able to have a discussion about personal space and the importance of having both "me" and "we" time. This is all contemplative thinking. Patty was also able to be assertive (and ask for what she wanted) rather than being domineering (and simply demanding it).

However, she wanted to see the current credit card bills for the two accounts that he had used when seeing the other woman.

"Not the past ones, the current bills. So I know nothing is happening still," she explained.

"That makes me feel checked up on, a small child that's not trusted," he said. "I'm completely transparent about my money. My salary comes right into our joint account."

I let the row continue, partly so all the feeling could come to the surface, but mainly to see if they could find their way back to contemplative thinking.

When Patty had expressed her distress and James had held her hand, she summed up the situation for both of them: "We are both tired and anxious about the future."

Once again, the atmosphere in the room was transformed by contemplative thinking. She had found some similarities between how they felt, and they could start to collaborate on James' forthcoming vacation and whether it could be used to provide time for both space and togetherness. I felt confident that they would find a formula where they both were satisfied—rather than producing a winner and loser (as in comparative thinking).

Learning how and when to use contemplative thinking is one of the three key skills for resolving your differences. I will return to the subject across the next two chapters.

5. Learning about yourself

I know your main attention has been on your partner because if he or she started acting reasonably then your relationship would be transformed and the crisis would be over. However, if your partner is depressed, you can't heal his or her illness. If your partner is besotted with his or her affair partner and considers them the great other, you are not going to reason the other man or woman out of their life. Even if your partner is neither depressed nor "in love" with someone else, you cannot control him or her. But you can learn a fundamental truth: *you can't change anybody but yourself.*

When Maggie stopped trying to manage her husband, she discovered that she could use all the saved time and energy to focus on herself. She decided to increase her hours at work and to improve her relationship with her daughter:

"In many ways, my husband and I had a division of labor with the children. He had a special relationship with our daughter and I had a special relationship with our son. So I've made a special effort to find mother and daughter bonding time. We've started baking together and it's amazing how many topics come up naturally in this unstructured time together."

There was another benefit. Instead of giving a day-by-day breakdown of her relationship with her husband over the past week, which took up about a third of our counseling sessions, we could use the saved time to go deeper. I reflected on how important it was to get her father's approval—even though she was an adult—and how her self-worth was tied up with what her husband thought of her.

"I've been thinking about the impact of my father on my character. Sometimes I hear his voice coming out of my mouth—particularly when I'm with my daughter."

"I was interested in how you're much closer to your son than your daughter—that you have 'valued' him more. Where does that come from?" I asked.

"My father! But how do I stop it?"

"You've made the first step by being aware. You're now less likely to pass on the legacy from the past."

Maggie nodded.

"You're also giving a lot of power to the men in your life," I noted. "First your father and then your husband. You could value yourself more highly rather than seek approval for them. After all, you are a strong, resourceful woman. How else would you have survived for so long with your husband undecided whether to stay or go?"

So how can you learn more about yourself? I would start by looking at your childhood—because the first messages that you were given about yourself and the world are always the most powerful—and see if there are patterns today that started back then. When Barack

Obama made his "A more perfect union" speech at the 2008 Democratic Party Conference—that marked him out as future political star—he paraphrased the American writer William Faulkner (1897–1962): "The past isn't dead and buried. In fact, it isn't even past." So thinking about this idea, what do you need to learn from the past?

There is a side bonus to working on yourself. If you change, there is a possibility that your partner might respond differently to you, and that could facilitate better communication (which in turn could break the deadlock between you). But even if your husband or wife remains mired in his or her depression or convinced of his or her love for a third party, learning about yourself is never wasted.

EXERCISE   MAKING A FULSOME APOLOGY

By this stage of the book, I hope that you have begun to look at your relationship with fresh eyes and now have a different take on your partner's behavior. I wonder if there is anything you regret doing or saying? Is there anything—if you had your time over—that you would do differently? If there is, this could form part of your apology.

I wouldn't be at all surprised if you are dismissive about apologies—you've apologized before and it's made hardly any difference. I wonder though if you've made a *fulsome* apology which is different from just saying: I'm sorry, with the accompanying explanation as to why you did what you did (see chapter five).

It's equally possible that an apology will stick in your throat. Just remember, apologizing does not put you in the wrong and your partner in the right. It just means that there is something that you regret, you're acknowledging the impact, and you're determined to avoid the same mistakes in the future.

In an ideal world it would feel better if your partner made the first move, but we don't live in an ideal world (and one of the benefits of being forty- or fifty-something is that we are mature enough to acknowledge this fact rather than howling at the moon that the world *should* be fair). If you're still unconvinced ... when your children fall out with each other or their friends, have you ever said: "Can you be the BIG ONE and apologize first?" Well, I'm asking you to be the big one now.

So what are the ingredients for a fulsome apology?

1. **Look at your behavior and make an honest assessment of the impact.** There is no point making an apology unless you mean it.

2. **Choose your time carefully.** It is pointless making a fulsome apology when you're angry. I would also avoid making one in the aftermath of a row as the specific issue of your disagreement could stop your partner from hearing a more general apology.

3. **Tell your partner what you regret.** For example, "I am sorry that I kept losing my temper," or "I am sorry that I was so inflexible over ...," or "I never realized how much you hated your job and the sacrifices that you made for us."

4. **Don't explain.** I know there are lots of good reasons why you behaved in this way. But at this point, explanations will be taken as excuses and lessen the power of your apology.

5. **Acknowledge the impact on your partner.** For example, "I realize that it did not make for a good atmosphere in the house/you felt controlled/you did not feel properly appreciated."

6. **Make a commitment to change.** Tell your partner about your plans to avoid falling into the same traps as before.

7. **Don't expect an immediate response.** If your partner wants to talk about what you've said—that's fine. If there is no response—that's fine too. Don't expect him or her to immediately apologize as well. Your partner probably needs time to digest what has been said. In general, I would keep any conversation short, so there is less likelihood of your olive branch being trampled underfoot.

DIFFERENCES BETWEEN A MAN AND A WOMAN GOING THROUGH MIDDLE PASSAGE

There is something about what society calls the midlife crisis that brings out a lot of comparative thinking. Sometimes it comes out as a judgmental question: "Why do men mess it up so spectacularly when they reach forty?" (There is often an unspoken assertion that women sail through their forties and fifties.) Sometimes the questions are more thoughtful: "Is it easier for a woman to make the transition?" or "What are the differences between a man coping with a wife who is depressed or having a midlife affair and a woman coping with the same situation with her husband?"

You won't be surprised that I try to answer these questions using contemplative thinking. It is hard being a wife coping with a husband who is a stranger *and* it is tough being a husband dealing with a wife acting out of character, too. The task of looking inward is challenging for men (who are trained to make a mark on the outside world). For women who are mothers, having children can change their entire outlook on life. As their sons and daughters move through the different life stages, mothers—usually the primary carers —have to adapt and their role changes. It could be that women are more prepared for change and better socialized to look at internal rather than external matters.

Still, I meet plenty of women who find it extremely hard to face up to unresolved issues from their childhood or to find a role as their children get older. I also know lots of women who loved their children dearly but being a mother was not the most important part of their identity.

I have also counseled couples where the husband gave up his career when the children were born. The stay-at-home fathers express the same concerns as stay-at-home mothers when the children are about to leave home—and often it is the working wives who are having the affairs. So here comes a very contemplative thinking approach ... On one hand, it might be the differing roles of being out in the world and being focused on the home that is at the root of destructive behavior, rather than gender. On the other hand, men and women are socialized differently and our culture has different expectations of them, and that is bound to have an impact during the middle passage.

Having said that, my main focus is to help *you* to deal with *your* partner's behavior. My policy, up to now, has been a unisex approach because the issues and the remedies are basically the same whatever your gender. And yet, there are differences between being a man and being a woman—so I think it would be helpful to address them (while at the same time noting that both you and your partner might not fit neatly into gender stereotypes).

The following idea comes from a study in the *New York Times* exploring the books, blogs, and social media presences created by mothers and fathers about the experience of being a parent. When I read the conclusion, it matched my experience of listening to mothers and fathers argue about childrearing over the past thirty years and provided a useful insight into the differences between how men and women view the world. So what was this revelation?

Fathers are looking for praise and mothers are looking for absolution. Staying with contemplative thinking, I think these statements are equally true for husbands and wives. Husbands do want applause (but women say: "Why should I congratulate him for emptying the dishwasher?"). Wives do want absolution (but men tend to blame their partners when things go wrong in their lives). Everybody needs to be appreciated and to feel special. Compliments and smiles cost nothing and go a long way. I understand that this might be difficult if positive reactions were rationed (or never used) when you were a child.

If I could change two things leading up to and during the middle passage, it would be to stop men from outsourcing the running of their emotional lives to their wives, and to get women to stop accepting the responsibility. It's up to each and every one of us to sort out our own lives (and that's a hard enough task without taking on a second load). Fortunately, at forty- or fifty-something, I hope that both you and your partner are ready to hear this message.

SUMMING UP

➤ It is incredibly difficult to cope with a partner going through the middle passage and nothing you have experienced up to now will have prepared you for it.

➤ I would not be surprised if your reactions to your partner's behavior have made the situation worse rather than better.

➤ If you can accept that both you and your partner are right, you have begun to use contemplative thinking. It will lay the foundation for listening better to each other and working as a team to find a way forward.

CHAPTER SEVEN

Dealing with depression and affairs

Armed with a better idea of what works (and what doesn't work) when your partner is going through the middle passage, I would like to think that the two of you will be ready to talk—really talk, to get to know who you are *today* (rather than who you were in the past or who you *thought* each other were), and begin to find a way forward. It is highly likely that there are two obstacles in the way: depression and an affair. I find they usually go hand in hand.

When Marie and Simon, both in their fifties, arrived in counseling, it was eighteen months since Simon had ended his nine-month affair with a work colleague.

"I've been to hell and back," explained Marie, "but I've stood by him—even though what he did makes no sense at all. However, I'm finally doing better. I've started to look after myself. I've got a little dog—who brings joy into my life—and I've been away on vacation with a girlfriend to recharge my batteries. It's Simon I'm worried about."

I could understand her concern. Simon was slumped on my couch and seemed to be carrying the cares of the world on his shoulders. When he spoke, there was no energy in his voice. "I don't recognize myself either," he told me.

"He comes from a very religious family, he was an altar boy, his brother is a priest, and we were married by the archbishop," Marie explained.

"What I did disgusts me," Simon sighed

It's a picture that I see over and over again: the shame that society, his wife, and children and his own conscience had piled onto Simon had replaced the temporary high of the affair with the pits of depression. In addition, even before the affair, Simon had been suffering from low-level depression.

"I suppose I wanted to be touched by someone who did not despise me," he said when we began to unpick some of the contributing factors for the infidelity.

"I did not despise you, we didn't always see eye to eye but that's different," chipped in Marie.

I am sure that she did not despise him, but in the toxic thinking of depression, even helpful suggestions like, "Don't forget to do your mindfulness exercises" can be heard as, "You're so stupid you can't even help yourself."

FIVE USEFUL THINGS TO SAY TO SOMEONE WITH DEPRESSION

There is plenty of advice about what *not* to say to someone depressed—like "pull yourself together" or (my personal bête noire) "man up"—but little on what might actually help. So I have looked at the blogs and books of people suffering with depression for inspiration. This is what these writers would *like* to have heard and the messages that, over time, helped.

1. What can I do to help?

When your partner is down and lacking in energy, it is tempting to step in and take over. A nurturing parent strategy can easily disempower (and remember, nurturing parent can easily tip over into critical parent mode). In contrast, asking what you can do to help keeps you firmly in the adult role and treats your partner as an adult (rather than a child).

It is perfectly possible that your partner will have no idea what he or she wants and if this is the case, simply add, "Let me know if you think of something." Even if your partner never accepts your offer, please keep offering because you are giving the unspoken message: "You are not alone."

2. You won't always feel this way

When someone is depressed, they find it hard to imagine that they will ever feel better. The gray today seems to merge into an endless blank future. By telling your partner, "You won't always feel this way," you are offering something that it is in short supply for him or her: *hope*.

There is another advantage: instead of trying to cheer your partner up (which can seem like you are trivializing the situation) you are acknowledging the problem. It's possible that you'll be met with a pile of woe. If this is the case, acknowledge what you've heard ("That sounds really hard") and be empathetic ("I'm sorry that you're so ... frustrated, angry, stressed," etc.)

The final advantage of "You won't always feel this way" is that it offers support without judgment, imposing, or manipulating.

3. I'm here for you

By using these words, you are preparing yourself to *listen* to your partner. Listening is one of the most powerful gifts that you can give someone (especially if they are depressed). If I had to sum up my work in one word, it would be *listening*. However, it is a special sort of listening. In the words of American poet Walt Whitman (1819–1892), "be curious, not judgmental." In this way, you will get an insight into the twisted logic of depression—without feeling the need to defend yourself or set your partner "right."

The statement "I'm here for you" also gives your partner a powerful message—that you support them, even if you might not understand how they feel. Therese J Borchard, the author of *Beyond Blue: Surviving depression & anxiety and making the most of bad genes*

(Center Street, 2010) says: "It's simple. It's sweet. And it communicates everything you need to say: I care, I get it, I don't really understand it, but I love you, and I support you."

4. Nothing

Saying nothing works on three different levels. First, and perhaps most important, it stops you feeling that you have to fix your partner's depression or your love will save him or her.

Second, it will help you to bite your tongue when your partner is snappy, critical, or angry. Although most people think depression is about sadness, it is also characterized by fatigue, disrupted sleep, distorted thinking, and—please remember this—irritability. If you can see your partner's mood-swings as part of his or her illness, it will be easier to let any hurtful comments go—rather than fighting back and making a bad situation worse. This can be particularly challenging if you have young children and your partner is easily stressed by childcare.

Third, actions can be more powerful than words. Rather than filling the gaps with chat about the weather or the kids, you could squeeze your partner's hand or sit with him or her while he or she watches a favorite TV program (especially if you don't like it).

5. Can you think of anything that's contributing to your depression at the moment?

If you thought saying nothing was difficult, this final strategy is even tougher and should only be used when you're over the worst of a crisis. (In the middle of an affair or a particular negative patch, you will probably get a list of all your failings—and, let's face it, you've probably heard enough about those already.)

However, if your partner is engulfed by shame in the aftermath of an affair, or dealing with generalized depression, this question can encourage the two of you to poke around at the current issues without pointing a stick at any one thing. For example, you might discover that your partner is dreading having to see your mother (who knows all about his or her affair) and is concerned about what she might say. Once your partner has identified the contributing factor, the two of you can begin to work out a strategy for dealing with it.

FIVE STRATEGIES TO HELP YOU LIVE WITH A DEPRESSED PARTNER

You've probably already discovered that it's really easy to make your partner more depressed, but really hard to improve his or her mood. I have five strategies that will help you to cope better (and which might have a positive knock-on effect on your husband or wife).

1. Patience

It goes without saying that it helps to be patient with your partner because depression is hard to overcome (and it can take a lot of time too). Nevertheless, living with someone who is depressed is tough and it can suck all the joy out of your home. So I would like you to extend the compassion that you try to feel—most of the time—toward your partner to yourself. It is difficult enough coping day to day without an internal critical voice commenting: "You shouldn't have done that" or "Now you've blown it" or "Why did you say that stupid thing?" So be patient with yourself, you will make mistakes, you will have breakthroughs and sometimes you will feel down too. It goes with the territory. Whatever happens, be patient with yourself.

2. Don't take things so personally

In most cases the patterns that lead to depression started long before you showed up. So think about your partner's childhood: did either of your partner's parents suffer from depression, how could his or her mother have contributed to the situation, what is the impact of the fathering that your partner received? Just because you're being handed the blame, doesn't mean you have to take it.

Even for day-to-day issues, it is probably not *"all* about you." Your children might have rubbed your partner up the wrong way, he or she might have not slept well, the day might be gray and unappealing. The list is endless.

3. Don't push your partner to seek help

When you see someone down—especially someone you love—you want to help. When you can't, you want them to seek professional help. After all, the doctor could prescribe antidepressants and a counselor could offer cognitive behavioral therapy (which you've heard is really good for depression). I know this all makes logical sense to you, but logic will not help. Your partner is living in a different universe and he or she has a critical internal voice (imagine the one in your head but more vicious) that can turn everything you say—however kind and thoughtfully intended—into an attack. So "Why don't you see the doctor?" turns into "You can't even get your act together to do something as simple as getting help." Your natural concern may be taken as proof that you don't have the first idea how bad he or she feels: "If you think the depths of my pain can be sorted by just talking …"

If you push it, your partner may only go to the doctor to get you off his or her back or to prove that you're wrong: "I told the doctor everything and she doesn't think I need medication."

There is also a danger that you could close down a possible avenue of help for the future.

Pushing for the professional help can be a sign of your magical thinking, by which I mean, hoping that one simple action will solve the whole problem. When the magical solution doesn't work—because resolving depression needs a wide range of complex interventions—you may tip into despair yourself.

4. It's not your job to make your partner better

I can't say this often enough. So I will say it again. You can't fix your partner. You are *not* responsible for his or her life (however much he or she wants to outsource the responsibility). Our society tell girls "Someday your prince will come" (to rescue you) and boys to go off and slay dragons (and thereby win the princess to be validated by her). These fairy-tales make more sense in the first half of our lives but not in the second. Obviously, there are more contemporary versions of these basic myths, but the same idea persists: the great other will save us.

As you're discovering, it's hard enough to sort out our own life—let alone someone else's. If you can accept what I'm saying—it's not your job to make your partner better—you'll begin to lift the weight of responsibility off your shoulders.

5. Look after yourself

When someone is ill in the family, the focus will be on looking after them. It's only natural and right. However, let's remember to use contemplative thinking: your partner has needs *and* you have needs too. Just because your partner's life is on hold due to their depression, it doesn't mean that your life needs to be too. So ask yourself: how can *I* stay on track with my life? How can *I* answer the central questions of the middle passage: Who am I? What gives my life meaning? What are my values? And: How can I fulfill *my* potential?

If your partner has sunk into depression following your discovery of their affair, you might have found the above strategies hard to swallow. How can you be patient when he or she has brought this on him or herself? When someone cheats on you, isn't that personal? After everything your partner has said and done, why should you put up with his or her snappiness and foul moods? If you're nodding along, this next element of looking after yourself is especially for you: setting good boundaries.

So what do I mean by boundaries? I have just stated one: you're not responsible for making your partner better. Boundaries are there to protect you (and to avoid setting yourself up for an impossible task and the inevitable pain of failing it). There are two ways of coping with a partner suffering from depression or in the aftermath of their affair. First, you could withdraw and build up your defenses (in other words, create high boundaries). Second, you could think: I need to get closer to my partner to sort everything out. So you dismantle your boundaries (or have low ones) and let him or her in again. In fact, you need a good enough boundary to protect yourself *and* you need to be open enough to create a new alliance to find a way out of this mess. This is contemplative thinking.

You need to protect yourself, to set limits regarding how much responsibility you're going to take on, and how much you're going to do for your partner. You might have to accept your partner's illness but not all the behaviors that go along with it. So, for example, if he or she is irritable and unreasonable, you need to explain how hurtful you find their comments or accusations. You're not going to respond to your partner's irritability with a counterattack (building up and defending your boundaries) and you're not going to just "suck it up" (low or no boundaries). You are going to have appropriate boundaries: honest communication which is assertive and adult to adult. (There is more about assertiveness in the next chapter.)

MY PARTNER IS DEPRESSED AND I'M ANXIOUS

One of the commonest pairings that I see in my counseling room is one partner who is depressed and the other who is anxious. So if your partner is depressed, I would not be at all surprised if you are anxious—especially if he or she has had an affair. After all, you will be anxious that it might be still be continuing behind your back or anxious about your partner being unfaithful in the future or anxious about being abandoned.

When Jermaine, forty-eight, had an affair for six months, his wife Toni, forty-seven, found the sexual betrayal particularly painful:

"For years I've wanted us to have a more sexually fulfilling life but whenever I'd spoken to Jermaine he's always said, 'I'll get round to it' but nothing happened. I thought he had a low libido or some medical problem. Now I discover, he had a perfectly healthy libido—just not with me," explained Toni.

Like all couples following the discovery of an affair, I helped Jermaine make a full disclosure and Toni to listen to him. We worked on improving communication and repairing their sex life. The affair had brought up unresolved issues from Jermaine's childhood and he was finding it hard to deal with his guilt and shame.

"I don't recognize the person who had this affair, I can't believe it's me and that's really frightening," he explained. "How could I do it?"

His tendency to procrastinate turned into lethargy and he started getting up later and getting less done. It seemed likely that Jermaine was depressed, so I suggested that he see his doctor who then made a formal diagnosis.

At first Toni was skeptical but read up on depression, found a better understanding of the illness, and accepted that he had not chosen to be depressed to avoid her anger.

It was a long haul. Jermaine did eventually take antidepressants which provided some temporary relief but the side-effects were debilitating. He stopped the medication, had some individual counseling and became strong enough to start working on his marriage again.

Toni still found it hard not to take Jermaine's behavior personally:

"Days will go by when he barely has enough energy to say hello and has the minimum interaction with me, but if a friend comes round, he's outgoing, sociable, and hasn't a care in the world."

"So why can you talk to friends and work associates but not to Toni?" I asked him.

"They're just light and unimportant topics and although I like my friends, I don't ultimately care what they think," Jermaine said.

In effect, he could handle low-grade conversations with unimportant people but not contentious topics with someone important to him like Toni.

"I know this is going to sound strange, but it's a backhanded compliment. He cares too much about the outcome of a discussion with you," I explained, and we started to focus on how to talk without it becoming a test for either Jermaine or Toni about the state of their relationship.

So if you're feeling anxious, how do you deal with it? The key is to accept it as healthy and normal. Unfortunately, our society wants to banish anxiety altogether. When I ask my clients to list the downsides of anxiety, they quickly come up with half a dozen answers. When I ask them to look at the advantages, they are stumped. So let me give you a couple of possibilities:

- If you feel anxious it means that you're on the edge of your comfort zone and that brings the possibility of change.

- If you never feel anxious, there is nothing at stake. (So if we somehow managed to create a world without anxiety, we would be trivializing the journey of life.)

- It is an early warning system that alerts you to a problem.

- Anxiety gives you nervous energy (preferable to depression, which drains you of vitality).

If you can accept anxiety as just one of a range of human emotions, you can begin to unpack it. There is a difference between fear (which is about something specific) and anxiety (which is more free-floating). In many cases, anxiety attaches itself to something that might never happen—for example, feeling anxious that your child might get run over if they walk to school on their own. If that's the case, you can begin to examine your thoughts and challenge them. Anxiety can be attached to unresolved problems from your childhood. Once you recognize this fact, you can begin to confront these issues as an adult (using the extra resources, knowledge, and skills that have been acquired growing up and from facing the challenges of the middle passage).

EXERCISE **BEING AND DOING**

There are two ways of approaching life: being *and* doing. I will explain the difference in a moment but first I wonder if you noticed how I set up this exercise. Rather than either/or (which is comparative), I used and/both (which is contemplative). I'm not saying that one is better than the other; they are just different. There are times when we need to "do" and times when we need to "be." If you are anxious or suffering from depression—because both have their roots in the same soil—you are probably spending more time doing rather than being.

Doing

Busy working through a list of tasks.

Working out what the problem might be.

Rumination leads to self-critical thoughts: what's wrong with me?

A temporary blip can spiral downward into a major incident.

Good at achieving goals and managing daily routines.

Can lead to "should" and "must" and believing "always" and "never."

On autopilot.

Leads to comparative thinking.

Being

Just experiencing the feelings.

Don't need to immediately find the cause.

Thoughts are events floating past, they don't have be taken seriously.

Living in the moment, not the past or the future, and open to the richness around me.

Being can access a deeper sense of knowing beyond what you can see and prove.

No longer trying to force life to be different because I'm comfortable with right now.

Aware.

Leads to contemplative thinking.

Over the next few days, monitor yourself and see how much time you spend "doing" and how much "being." What is the impact of each approach on your general welfare? How could you find a balance that works better for you?

MY PARTNER IS HAVING AN AFFAIR

The problem with dealing with an affair is not so much the betrayal (which is bad enough) but that all the lying and deceit has destroyed your trust. You don't know what to believe. Has the affair ended or are the "lovers" still in contact? Does your partner still love you or is he or she just saying it? When you don't know where you stand, your anxiety levels will go through the roof and it's highly possible that you'll say and do things you regret (and which your internal critical voice then uses as a stick to beat you with and creates further anxiety).

In an ideal world, your partner would have realized just how destructive, on so many levels, an affair can be before he or she set off on this course of action. In the same world, he or she would have had the skills to speak up about any unhappiness, rather than burying it and becoming vulnerable to temptation. Once the affair was discovered, he or she would have made immediate steps to remedy the situation—rather than minimize what really happened and still be economical with the truth. Sadly, we don't live in this ideal world, so let's look at the three common scenarios postdiscovery of an affair and how to deal with them.

My partner is ashamed and apologetic

Most of the time, your partner makes all the right noises. He or she is deeply ashamed of his or her behavior and wants to puts things right but can get defensive and angry—especially when you can't "move on," too, or when you want to talk about some aspect of the affair.

What this says about your situation: my guess is that the affair is over. Your partner might have moments of weakness—for example when he or she checks the affair partner's Facebook page—but these are blips rather than a major setback (unless you turn them into one). Your partner would genuinely like to save your marriage but, like you, is worried about whether that's possible or not.

Going forward: Affairs go through seven stages from discovery to recovery. They are Shock and Disbelief, Intense Questioning, Decision Time, Hope, Attempted Normality, Despair, and Intense Learning. Understanding the stages—and how you can slip back down the ladder—is really helpful. This stops you from panicking and thinking your relationship is doomed when, in reality, you're just going through a natural phase. Don't worry if you don't trust your partner now as that doesn't come back until you've been through all seven stages. (There is more help in my book *How Can I Ever Trust You Again?*)

My partner is all over the place

One moment, your partner is begging for another chance, and the next, declaring the relationship over. He or she goes through phases of buying presents or being especially nice and then acting cold, dismissive and cruel. You feel like you're treading on eggshells and don't know quite what to expect from one moment to the next. In the worst-case scenario, your partner will leave saying they need "space" or because he or she "can't live without" the affair partner, but returns a few days or weeks later. There are promises of a new start but nothing has fundamentally changed.

What this says about your situation: Your partner is torn between his or her concern for you (plus wanting the best for the children) and his or her new love. Even if he or she has decided to stay, which seems positive, he or she is still keeping the door open for the affair partner (in case things don't work out) or just mourning for what could have been. Whatever the background, it is deeply upsetting and destabilizing and stopping you both from healing.

Going forward: You are stuck in the drama triangle of victim, persecutor, and rescuer which I introduced in chapter four. Although a triangle is the strongest shape—used in bridges because it can take a lot of weight—none of the roles are stable and it is easy to shift from victim (after all you've been betrayed) to persecutor (cross-questioning your partner late into the night) and rescuer (where you forgive him or her and want to start again). Similarly, the affair partner will see her or himself as rescuing your husband or wife from your persecution, which makes you the abuser (for keeping the "lovers" apart) and your partner the victim. Finally, your partner will, at times, feel the victim (because he or she was unhappy and unattended to in the marriage) and also the abuser (for being unfaithful) but will become the rescuer to make you feel better (for a while).

The only way to break a triangle is for one of the players to withdraw. Back in my ideal world, the affair partner would realize his or her mistake and let go, but if he or she has deep-seated issues and believes love will save the day, he or she is likely to hold on to your partner with a grip of steel. Your partner may be unable to make a decision.

I know none of the options are appealing at the moment. However, if you're fed up with the drama triangle, consider setting up a temporary separation. It could deter your partner from walking out in desperation or stop you from throwing him or her out during a row. (There is more advice about temporary separations in the next chapter.)

My partner is defiant and unapologetic

Your partner says he or she is sorry for upsetting you, but does not regret the affair. He or she might even refuse to answer questions because it is "none of your business." Although your husband or wife doesn't text the affair partner under your nose, he or she does very little to hide their continuing communication. From your husband's or wife's viewpoint, if you're upset that's *your* problem because you should accept the situation and "get a life."

What this says about your situation: While you are tying yourself in knots to save your marriage, your partner has left it. He or she has looked at the complexity of being forty- or fifty-something and, rather than facing the issues, has fled into the arms of someone else. You could try and reason with them, but just as you wouldn't expect sense out of someone who was drunk, it's the same with someone under the influence of limerence.

Going forward: Your partner will continue to be untrustworthy. He or she may agree not to say anything to his or her parents, for example before the big family party for their golden wedding anniversary, and then break his promise—leaving you embarrassed and angry and coping with your in-laws' pity. Take everything your partner says with a bucket load of salt. He or she is under the influence of a third party who is no friend to your marriage, your children, and most definitely not to you. Basically, you have two choices—either to make a tactical withdrawal (hoping your partner will eventually come to his or her senses) or go straight for mediation or a divorce. With both options, it is important that you disengage to protect your own sanity. (See my previous books *My Husband Doesn't Love Me and He's Texting Someone Else* and *My Wife Doesn't Love Me Anymore* for further advice on how to make a tactical withdrawal.)

EXERCISE   A BALANCED VIEW OF INFIDELITY

When your partner is having or has had an affair, it is very tempting to fall into comparative thinking. In the media, couples are usually divided into the guilty party (the cheater) or the innocent party (who was cheated on). From here we're straight into the territory of right or wrong and good or bad and it's all downhill to blaming and shaming. It also places you in the victim role and your partner in the abuser role and keeps you both stuck in the drama triangle. So to move toward a more balanced view of infidelity, I would like to consider the many ways of betraying a marriage without cheating:

- Telling little white lies to avoid conflict.

- Forming a coalition against your partner. (Sometimes with all the children, but I often see mothers becoming especially close to their sons and fathers to their daughters.)

- Absenteeism or coldness.

- Withdrawal of sexual interest.

- Disrespect. (This can include shaming comments or a contemptuous/superior attitude.)

- Selfishness. (Getting your own way all the time.)

- Breaking promises.

- Self-righteousness. (Believing your way, for example of bringing up the children, must be followed at all times.)

How many of these traps did your partner fall into before the affair? What about you? So how would it change the atmosphere in your house if you moved from comparative into contemplative thinking: Your partner has made mistakes *and* you have made mistakes (albeit different ones).

HEALING FROM AN AFFAIR

A middle passage affair is particularly hurtful. In your forties and fifties, you and your partner are at a vulnerable age. He or she will find the lure of the great other stronger, and the chemistry more combustible, and the chance of he or she leaving (if only temporarily) is therefore higher. Your confidence will be lower—noting younger rivals at work, and younger men and women turning heads—and so the sexual betrayal feels greater and the wound deeper. It follows that the job of healing takes longer and the approach needs to be more profound.

Fortunately, there is one big advantage to being forty- or fifty-something: You are more able to look beneath pleasant surfaces and peer into dark corners. My clients often tell me that they would rather have kept their "innocent" view of life—but this only serves us well in the first half. By the second half, we're ready to face the complexity. There is one more piece of good news: a greater understanding of relationships leads to a better recovery and ultimately to a deeper capacity for love.

The two wounds of every childhood

When you were young, the world will have appeared big and you will have felt small. Psychologists believe this experience gives us two basic wounds. The first is called the wound of *being overwhelmed* and is caused by the puzzling environment around us (parents, older siblings, school, and the forces beyond—including socioeconomic influences and what fate throws at us, like our parents' divorce, illness, death, etc.). The second wound is *being insufficient*. As small children, we had little power or agency in the world (no credit card or car keys) but our parents could not always be there for us. Therefore we grow up full of unfulfilled desires but cannot fully rely on the world to meet our needs. So how do we cope with the wounds of *being overwhelmed* and *insufficient*? We use one or a combination of the following strategies:

1. *Overcompensate.* You try to seize control or gain power through your looks or being clever, in order to accumulate wealth, fame, success, etc. Unfortunately, you risk becoming bossy (gaining overt power) or manipulative (seeking to gain covert power). On the surface, you will seem confident but this can hide a feeling of inner powerlessness or lack of self-worth.

2. *Anxious accommodation.* This coping strategy is basically "give them what they want," even if it overrides your own needs. It involves obsessively following the rules and hoping that if you please the people who seem to be in control, they will pull the levers of power for your benefit. Unfortunately, in order to boost your self-worth you are always seeking the reassurance of others.

3. *Avoidance*. Instead of dealing with the world, you retreat, disassociate, procrastinate, and attempt to diminish your responsibility by blaming others. This strategy often leads to self-sabotage. In a way, not asking for anything can seem a position of strength (because there is no rejection or disappointment) but, in reality, you can feel worthless and unlovable.

Use this knowledge to heal: When Lloyd, fifty-three, became friendly with his language tutor while working abroad, he kept the closeness of his relationship back from his wife, Brenda, and he lied about exchanging texts and meeting up for the odd lunch.

"When the affair was uncovered, he looked me in the eye and repeatedly lied, claiming it was only one telephone call and six texts," explained Brenda. "There are all sorts of details that don't make sense, so I wonder if he's still lying."

Brenda seemed stuck in the first two stages of recovery: Shock and Disbelief and Intense Questioning. Three months after the original discovery, she was still regularly gripped with panic and nausea. "Even though I know I will only hurt myself, because I feel so desperate afterward, I will cross-question him—sometimes till two in the morning. I don't sleep properly and it's the first thing on my mind when the alarm goes off."

When I looked into Brenda's childhood, I found that her mother had a very close relationship with her sister while Brenda felt excluded.

As I had suspected, it was the holding back of the information—rather than the betrayal of the emotional affair—that hurt her the most.

"It's like you've been excluded again. It seems today's pain has triggered echoes of a more profound and deeper one from your childhood," I told her.

Brenda had coped with her wound of feeling insufficient by *anxious accommodation* and hoped that by being a good girl she would win her mother's affection. As the patterns set in our childhood are often carried over into our provisional adulthood (the first half of our life), it is not surprising that she had put a lot of store in being a good wife. So when this strategy failed to keep her husband emotionally faithful (or even honest), she was completely floored and had, instead, started to *overcompensate* (by needing to know and control everything).

When I looked at Lloyd's life, I found that both his father and his sister had died young, so when he felt the wounds of being overwhelmed (by the depths of his wife's pain) and insufficiency (because he had no adequate response for why he did it or full recall about particular details of the affair timeline), he responded with his own childhood strategy—*avoidance*—which further compounded Brenda's pain.

Although explaining the origins of their crisis did not resolve the pain, it did help Brenda and Lloyd understand the situation better. Brenda stopped feeling like she was "going mad" and Lloyd stopped thinking she was "overreacting". He also tried to check himself when he started to disassociate from her. Slowly but surely, they began to move through the rest of the stages of recovery.

Look through spiritually attuned eyes

I've been asking you to look under the surface of your relationship at the greater mysteries of life. Your partner's crisis has meant that unresolved problems from the past—both his or hers and yours too—have come up to the surface. I want to reassure you that addressing these problems will enlarge your life, not diminish it. You may not want to change and grow but life is asking more of you than that. With this idea in mind, here are some questions to help in the task of looking through spiritually attuned eyes:

What brought you to this place in your journey through life? It might be easier to blame your partner, but that abdicates personal responsibility and limits your choices for the future.

What messages, myths, and forces have shaped your reality? Sometimes these might have supported your life journey and sometimes they will have been constricting. Does it feel that the script to your life was written elsewhere without you really being consulted? Have you obeyed everyone else's instructions to the best of your ability, but even when things are going well, they do not feel quite right? Are you living a life too small for your soul's desire?

What have you learned—however unwanted—through coping with your partner's crisis? To quote an old proverb, "When life gives you lemons, make lemonade." In other words, if you can find something positive out of an experience it will make the pain more bearable. What else do you need to learn?

Why is now the time to accept a summons to live a second larger life? My guess is that you and your partner have used old scripts and ways of relating to each other. Isn't it time to try something new?

SUMMING UP

- ➢ It is not your job to heal your partner.

- ➢ Depression is a sedative but anxiety can be an elixir that keeps you on the edge of your life.

- ➢ If you can turn the pain into something to help you grow, you can change your experience from a negative into a positive one.

CHAPTER EIGHT

A new approach

At the moment, your partner may see you as the enemy and believe that you want to trap him or her in your old life together (or a close approximation of it). If things have gone from bad to worse, your partner will feel you're standing in the way of his or her true happiness. My goal is turn the current situation on its head: to help you be on his or her team and for the two of you to find a way forward together. In this chapter, I'm going to explain how.

I wouldn't be surprised if you have already tried to help your partner or bring him or her to the negotiating table but have been met with a brick wall or some killer reason why any dialogue is pointless. So before you can start to use the ideas I've begun to outline and the skills you've started to hone, you need to get past these blocks.

FIVE REASONS PEOPLE USE FOR GIVING UP ON THEIR RELATIONSHIP

I've heard hundreds of reasons from unhappy people as to why they believe their relationship is beyond saving. Essentially they boil down to five main reasons for giving up. Fortunately, I have five counterarguments that you might find useful.

I can't change my feelings

Sometimes this message is softened, for example, "If I could flick a switch in my head, I would" and sometimes it is very direct, "I don't love you any more and all the talking in the world won't change that."

Turn it around: In your partner's mind, feelings are fixed and immovable. In fact, he or she *used* to love you and if the feelings changed once (from positive to negative), there is the potential for them to change again. I know it is tempting to point this out to your partner but I've seldom found that it works. Most probably because your partner is speaking from the heart and this is an intellectual response.

My suggested reply would be: "I don't want you to change your feelings. If you're feeling this way it is probably for a good reason and I'd like to know more." In most cases, you'll discover your partner is angry, resentful, sad, depressed, or bitter. All these feelings need to be aired and accepted before the good ones can be released.

In my opinion, feelings are like a river and if you unblock the unexpressed emotions, the water will start to flow again. Although the first feelings down the mountainside may be upsetting and disturbing, by letting them flow you will have a better understanding of the problems, the beginnings of a dialogue, and finally some hope too.

I don't fancy you any more

This is not only hard to hear—because it makes you feel more rejected and less attractive—but your relationship sounds doomed. If you don't fancy someone, how can you have sex again? Who wants to spend the rest of their life in a brother/sister-type relationship?

Turn it around: The temptation is to recall how good sex used to be (in the hope that it will make your partner believe in your relationship again), but this strategy just reminds him or her of how poor or nonexistent your lovemaking is *now*. So I would suggest this reply: "I'm not surprised. Anger and low-level resentment is the biggest turn-off in the world." Once the anger is expressed, rather than bottled up, it has the opportunity to burn out. At this point, and only then, can you begin to truly see each other again (and maybe start to like each other and finally to feel desire again).

It is often men who say "I don't fancy you any more" because they feel in some way responsible for sex (and one of the myths fed to them is that they have to be ever ready and up for it). I consider sex to be a *joint* responsibility. Rather than a man having to feel desire and then approach his partner and initiate sex, a couple can kiss, cuddle, and fondle each other and generate their desire together.

I can't see a way forward

It's not so much that your partner can't see a solution—because you've probably laid out hundreds—but he or she doesn't *believe* in them. Either consciously or unconsciously, he or she is worried about being unable to deliver a new-look relationship between you and hurting you (and him or herself) all over again.

Turn it around: My suggestion is to acknowledge your partner's doubts, to talk about your own, and communicate the message that it's OK to have doubts. In fact, I would go a step further and say it is *good* to have doubts. They will encourage you to take your time, check in with each other, and constantly refine the way forward (so it works for both of you). I'm more concerned if someone is completely certain as it normally means that they are repressing doubts, desperately trying to convince themselves (as much as their partner), and marching straight toward a brick wall. In effect, doubts can be your friend.

What about your partner being "frightened of hurting you again?" In my mind, this sounds like your partner is in nurturing parent mode and you've been placed in the adapted child role (about to stamp your feet because you were promised a trip to the fair). I would prefer that you were both in the adult mode, especially when you negotiate, because adults understand that things come up which make it impossible to go the fair on a particular day; and that "no" means "not now" rather than "never." What's more, an adult can accept a raincheck, a different excursion, a shorter trip to the fair, or a pact to avoid the roller-coaster.

We're different people

In some ways, this message is kinder and easier to hear because it does not put the blame on anybody. Your partner believes you want different things and there is, therefore, no future together.

Turn it around: Instead of trying to list your similarities or just flatly contradicting your partner, my suggestion would be to agree: "Being different is pushing us apart at the moment but it could be an asset." How can this be? Two heads are better than one and two approaches can produce a creative tension that brings better results. This is particularly the case when your differences begin to balance each other and provide a middle way. For example, with your finances, two spenders would end up with huge debts while two savers wouldn't have much fun. A balanced couple would be both financially responsible and enjoy their money.

You're too controlling

There is no getting away from the fact that this is extremely critical and the natural response is to get upset (because who wants to be branded as controlling by their partner) or to be puzzled (because you don't recognize this picture of yourself) or to go on the attack (and list your partner's faults). Unfortunately, all three approaches put another brick in the wall between the two of you and confirm your partner's belief that talking is not only pointless but actually makes matters worse.

Turn it around: Instead of getting angry, I would like you to thank your partner for being assertive with you. I know this sounds a strange response, but a lack of honesty is the crux of why some relationships self-destruct during the middle passage. Don't worry, I am not saying that you *are* controlling but that your partner *perceives* that you are. So what's going on? If your partner wants to be liked or tends to appease people, it may have been hard for him or her to say "you're too controlling"—hence my request to thank him or her. This gives you *both* a chance to work on the most important tool for recovery: being assertive with each other.

THE POWER OF ASSERTIVENESS

If I had to give just one reason why some marriages are destroyed by the middle passage while some are deepened, strengthened, and enhanced, I would put it down to how couples handle conflict. Before I outline the three different ways of handling your differences, I would like to give an example from my case book to illustrate what someone means when they accuse their partner of being controlling, what's really going under the surface, and how assertiveness can turn the situation around.

Frank, forty-four, had used all five reasons for giving up on his ten-year marriage with his wife, Ann, forty-one. By the time they started counseling, Frank had settled down on "we're different people" and the evidence for this was that Ann was being "too controlling."

"I work away during the week and I'd hardly got in through the door from Friday-night traffic, before we'd had a row. It's hopeless," he sighed.

"But I'd got the children to bed, cleared everything up, and lit a fire so you felt welcome and could relax," said Ann.

"So why did you say, 'I've got the wood-burning stove going without making a mess?'"

"It was just an observation."

"And then you complained about me walking mud into the house."

"I'm just asking for you to be considerate because it's me that has to clear everything up," she said.

At this point, Frank looked around the carpet in my office and pointed to a piece of dark wool against the light carpet:

"It was probably five times worse than that," he said in an exasperated way.

"You're just exaggerating now," she countered.

"I rest my case," he said. "There is just one way to run the stove—Ann's way. There is just one level of cleanliness—hers—and it does not make for relaxed family time. I feel unheard, dominated, and bullied by her controlling nature."

"I wonder if his snide undermining comments and nagging could add up to bullying too," Ann countered.

The battle lines had been clearly drawn up and the chances of them working as a team to resolve their differences seemed remote. So how had they got to this impasse?

Passive and domineering

If Ann was as controlling as Frank was suggesting, it seemed incredible that he had lasted for ten years with her before seeking help. So I asked him about it.

"If the situation is as bad as you've presented it, how have you survived for so long?"

"I've just bitten my lip, but I've had enough and now I've snapped," he said.

In other words, when faced with conflict—over two ways of running the wood-burning stove—he had been passive. By passive, I mean: *My needs, beliefs, and opinions are of lesser importance and your needs, beliefs, and opinions are of supreme importance.* I know this makes Frank, and other people like him, sound a complete doormat. On a superficial level, they tell themselves, "It's not worth getting bent out of shape over a wood-burning stove"—and they're right—but if you downgrade your needs too often it becomes not a choice but a habit and ultimately a way of life. On a deeper level, passive people believe that the best way to get their needs met—in his case for a quiet life and to be loved—is to go along with what other people want. They have an unspoken contract with the world: "You scratch my back, and I'll scratch yours."

Unfortunately, while Frank was biting his lip Ann had no idea that he was truly unhappy or how resentful he was becoming. Worse still, she had no idea what he really wanted because he had never stated his needs clearly or only in an argument (when it can be dismissed as something nasty said in the heat of the moment). The result was that Ann, to stay with the metaphor, had no idea that Frank needed his back scratched or how bad the itch had become. When his unspoken contract had been not delivered, Frank flipped over into the other side of the passive coin: being domineering.

So what is domineering? Basically it is the opposite of passive: *My needs, beliefs, and opinions are of supreme importance and yours are of lesser importance.* In effect, Frank had decided that "life" or Ann owed him. Therefore he (albeit unconsciously) decided that his needs, beliefs, and opinions had become paramount while Ann's were of lesser significance. He had started to spend time with people whom he described as "more like myself," which included ex-partners, women with whom he exchanged sexually provocative messages, and female work colleagues who offered "personal support." Ann's need for a husband who was supportive and attentive had been effectively downgraded and then trumped by Frank's needs.

Domain-specific control

Although Frank thought their marriage had survived because he had downgraded his needs, the picture was more complicated. With a little digging, I discovered that Frank and Ann had found a sort of balance where he was domineering (in control) in some areas, while she was passive (downgrading her needs) in others, and vice versa. When it came to money and his job, Frank was in charge (he had chosen to work away) and Ann had to bite her lip (even though she felt abandoned and unsupported during the week). Meanwhile when it came to the house (level of cleanliness) and the children (how they would be brought up), Ann was in charge and Frank bit his lip and

225

carried out her instructions (and if he disagreed she'd overrule him with pages of "evidence" from the Internet).

These kinds of arrangements can work for years until something unsettles the balance. It could be the arrival of the second child, the breadwinner losing his or her job, bereavement, going through the middle passage, or perhaps caring for an infirm parent, but one partner will feel controlled (like Frank) while the other person remains mystified by their reactions (like Anne).

If you have been accused of being controlling, your first reaction would probably have been anger, but once that had lessened, I would expect you to be truly puzzled. So why would this be? It is human nature that you will remember your losses more than your wins—particularly if you settle disputes through domain-specific control. For example, Ann will remember her loneliness during the week and overlook that the children go to bed when she decides. She might not even register that their bedtime on Friday night was her choice; after all, it was in the children's best interests to get a good night's sleep (and all right-thinking people would agree with her). Maybe the idea that they could stay up late on Fridays to see their father might not even have crossed her mind. If Frank had never spoken up—and followed through, which is even more important—about the children's bedtime on Friday nights, Ann would not have known that it was a contentious issue.

Being assertive

If being passive is when you consider your partner's needs of greater importance and being domineering is when your needs are important and your partner's less so, being assertive is when *both* of your needs, beliefs, and opinions are *equally* important. That's fine if you both want the same thing but what happens if you want, for example, to go out and your partner wants to stay in?

The solution is to negotiate and find a solution both of you can live with. It could be a compromise (we'll only go out for a short while), a trade (I'm staying in with you, if you use the time to fix the light in the hallway) or a concession. What do I mean by a concession? Your partner makes a good case for staying in (for example, he or she has to get up early) or you make a good case for going out (for example, we can meet up with friends we haven't seen for a long time) or that one of you decides to back down. However, conceding only works if enough time and care is taken so that *both sides feel heard*. With assertiveness, instead of a winner and a loser you have two people who are happy with the outcome: two winners.

Returning to James and Patty whom we met in chapters one and six, their counseling worked because of one simple change each of them made. James learned that it was OK to have different needs, beliefs, and opinions from Patty (and the world would not end if they disagreed). This allowed James to become a proper advocate for his needs. In other words, he stopped being passive. Meanwhile Patty learned to be more flexible (and the world would not end if the way she thought was not followed). In other words, she had stopped being domineering. The result was that they could become assertive and negotiate a middle way, trade, or concede. It took time and a couple of false starts—where James would offer compromises that he knew Patty would like but which left him feeling short-changed. I knew they had had a breakthrough when they reported how they had allocated their time over the Christmas/New Year holiday.

"Patty's family lives on the other side of the world so it's not worth going there just for a few days," James explained. "We'd agreed to take a vacation let—rather than stay with one branch of the family — so we had couple time too. When I didn't feel like going over to her brother and sister-in-law for supper one evening, I spoke up and Patty was fine about going on her own."

"But when he wanted to skip my brother's big New Year's Eve party I knew my family would be upset," Patty said.

"Patty's brother and his wife have a lot of superrich friends, which makes me feel uncomfortable, but Patty and I reached a compromise where we would leave early if the party was boring," said James. "However, I found a couple of guys who also liked fishing so we had that in common. The food was outstanding and we ended up spending longer at the party than planned."

James' need to enjoy his vacation and Patty's need to spend time with her family *and* be with her husband on New Year's Eve were equally important. By being assertive, they had not only found a way of meeting both their goals but a way of dealing with conflict. They had integrated my assertiveness maxim—"I can ask, you can say no (or maybe) and we can negotiate"—into their everyday lives. Slowly but surely they went from solving smaller dilemmas, like how to spend New Year's Eve, onto bigger ones—like "Are we ready to live together again?"

EXERCISE   STAND DOWN SOLDIER

During the Second World War, the Japanese Imperial Army stationed soldiers on remote islands in the Pacific and deep in the jungles of the region. In the chaos of the end of the war, the authorities either forgot where they had left their warriors, records were destroyed, or the men had gone so far underground that they couldn't be found. Therefore many soldiers, unaware of defeat, kept on fighting and in one famous case, Hiroo Onoda, an intelligence officer, fought for twenty-nine years after the Japanese army had surrendered.

So why am I telling you this story? It provides a good metaphor for what has been happening to your partner. Let me explain the parallels. In many ways, getting yourself established in your teens, twenties, and early thirties is a bit like a war. You have to be focused on passing exams, finding a job, climbing the career ladder, finding a partner, and setting up home. In each of these rites of passage, there is competition from countless other people who want to be top of the class, get the internship or land the first job, become a junior partner, marry the most popular man or woman, and buy the house in the catchment area for the right school. It truly can feel like a battle zone. Extending the metaphor, the generals are our parents and society who give us the messages to succeed, make them proud, be happy, etc. We need their simple "one size fits all" rules to control our less civilized impulses, and without goals, rules, and authority figures, our inner soldier would have been directionless, undisciplined, and lack the ability to form sustained relationships.

But as I've explained already, what is right for the first half of our life is not necessarily right for the second half. We don't need to be focused on winning all the time. We need to discover who we are—rather than follow the commands, or what we thought were the commands—of our parents and society (and maybe our partner too).

Returning to the Japanese soldiers, in the beginning the authorities simply told them the war was over, that they were citizens again, and provided transport back home. Unfortunately, these men didn't always believe what they were told. They were confused, angry, depressed, or got into trouble. Does this sound familiar?

Fortunately, the Japanese created a ritual to help these soldiers to "stand down." A former high-ranking soldier would take out his old uniform, go to the island in an old military boat, and enter the forest calling out the soldier's name. When they met, the officer would thank the solider for his loyalty, often with tears in his eyes, and praise his courage. The officer would ask about his experiences and only then explain Japan was at peace and he no longer needed to fight. This ritual helped the returning soldiers make the transition from warrior to a broader identity (and therefore return to normal society).

What I'm suggesting is a ritual to thank your partner's inner soldier for all the hard work put in to getting to this point in your lives together, and to help him or her in the transition from part one to part two of his or her life.

How it works

Here is my ritual for helping your partner's inner soldier to stand down:

- Choose your moment carefully. This ritual works best when things are on a reasonably even keel. If you are in the makeup phase after an argument, your partner might be too angry to hear you or your message might be heard as "trying to get back into my good books" and the power diluted.

- I will provide a rough script for the first part but the rest has to come from your heart. It helps if you have taken some time to think through your message.

- Start by saying something like "I don't know if I have ever thanked you properly for everything you do and have done for me and the children. So I wanted to tell you what I admire about you and what I'm particularly grateful for."

- Go through the qualities for which you'd like to thank your partner. For example, generosity, capacity for hard work, determination, etc.

- Come up with a couple of examples of tasks or jobs that your partner does. For example, planning vacations, organizing social life, cooking, running a welcoming home.

- Honor some particular achievements. For example, "I admire how you dealt with being out of work five years ago" or "how you cared for my mother when she was ill" or "providing this wonderful house that is a sanctuary for us all."

- Try and be as specific as possible—rather than just "great father or mother," think of qualities your partner possesses and a couple of examples.

- It might be embarrassing for your partner to receive praise—particularly if he or she did not get it as a child—so don't be disheartened if he or she brushes it aside. Simply reply: "I know you're modest and I like that too but I think it's important to tell you these things from time to time."

- If your partner is a man, the task is relatively simple as men are generally looking for *praise*. My advice would be to focus on what a good provider he has been and how much you appreciate it. For most men, providing is central to their cultural identity, so you will be pressing all the right buttons. In the second half of his life, it might be helpful for your husband to share more of the responsibility for providing and free himself to discover a broader identity.

- If your partner is a woman, the message needs to be more nuanced as women are generally looking for *absolution*. My advice would be to tell her that she is NOT responsible for your unhappiness or infidelity (as at some level, she will blame herself). I would also praise her for bringing up such well-rounded children—especially if her own childhood was problematic or her own mother was difficult, as she may have been wary of history repeating itself. Even if she had a great childhood and a straightforward relationship with her mother, modern society often blames any problems with children on poor mothering (and at some level, your wife will fear this is true).

- Finally, I would spend most of this ritual going back over old campaigns (or joint projects) and what you have achieved together—as this builds teamwork. Be careful not to turn the ritual of thanks into reasons to stay together as this will lessen the power of your message (as your partner will think the praise has an ulterior motive).

NORMAL RESISTANCES

I wouldn't be surprised if right now you're saying, "Yes, but ..." Here are the most common reasons why you may skip the above exercise, along with my thoughts on each one:

■ *My partner knows I appreciate him or her.* First, I am sure that this is true but I can't tell you how much it meant to me when my partner once thanked me, for no particular reason, for my generosity and for being a good provider. (That helped to inspire this exercise.) Second, when people use this reason I'm reminded of an old saying: *Nobody thinks they are paid enough.*

■ *I shouldn't have to thank my partner for doing anything; that's part of the deal of being married.* It sounds like praise is rationed in your household or if one person gets praised, someone else is overlooked. My guess is that praise seemed a scarce resource when you were growing up because you got so little of it. Or maybe praise came with strings. However, when *praise comes from the heart*, it does not come with conditions and because there is no worldwide shortage of praise, it can be given freely.

- *My partner does not deserve to be praised.* If you have just discovered some particularly cruel behavior by your partner, it is probably not the time for this ritual. Even if you are on a reasonably even keel, saying thank you for one behavior does not mean that you endorse another. Telling your partner what you appreciate about him or her—rather than what you hate—could be the turning point in relations between the two of you.

HOW TO USE CONTEMPLATIVE THINKING TO TURN ROUND YOUR RELATIONSHIPS

In chapter six, I explained how our world revolves around comparative thinking and how we understand the world by labeling, judging, and dividing. With this approach, we end up with:

Good vs Bad

Right vs Wrong

Wise vs Stupid

Winner vs Loser

Success vs Failure.

The result, according to writer and Franciscan monk Richard Rohr, is a dualistic mind which readily falls into the six Cs of delusion: Compares, Competes, Conflicts, Conspires, Cancels out any contrary evidence, and Crucifies with impunity. As I've explained, there is another approach, contemplative thinking, where instead of either/or you accept that the world is not black vs white (which is another classic comparative divide).

Please be aware that I don't want to set up a dualistic mindset with comparative vs contemplative thinking where one is wrong and the other right. Comparative thinking was fine when you were defining yourself as teenager—and with heroic thinking you were convinced of your own innate superiority. Of course your chosen soccer team, music tastes, country, religion, or ethnic group was better than mine. By dividing who was in and who was out you had a clearer sense of self.

In the second half of our life, we need a wider frame or we get stuck with "my facts are better than your facts" and "my shoulds are stronger than your shoulds." As you've discovered, your partner has probably used comparative thinking to crucify you (and, if it's not going to make you too angry, you've probably been describing his or her behavior as "bad," which allows you to do your own share of crucifying too). As you're discovering, comparative thinking is not helpful for the big issues of the second half of life: love, suffering, death, finding meaning, and spirituality.

I know you are going to have doubts about giving up comparative thinking. You're going to say something like: "Surely some things are simply wrong—like cheating on your partner" or "Ultimately, don't you have to decide one way or another?" The other accusation I get is that you will end up with mushy or relative thinking where anything goes. I welcome doubts because they are just a staging post along the way. All I ask is that, for the moment, you hold both your doubts and your curiosity at the same time. To use contemplative thinking: you are concerned that what I'm advocating leads nowhere AND I might have something useful to break the deadlock between you and your partner.

The three stages of contemplative thinking

When couples start counseling, they arrive believing that "one of us is wrong and it's certainly not me" (or occasionally "one of us is wrong and, guess what, it's me"). My overarching aim is to take them through the following three stages to find a resolution for their problems:

Opening: You need to open your mind and bypass comparative thinking—for the time being. After all, concepts like "good" and "bad" are just labels. For example, anger might seem bad because it can breed aggression and rows, but it can provide a sense of urgency that something needs to change.

If you have begun opening up to these ideas, you can start to embrace paradoxes—by which I mean ideas that initially look contradictory but by using a different frame of reference can become true. For example: *the best way to fall back in love is to have an argument.* I know it sounds contradictory, but a *constructive* argument (by that I mean no personal attacks, switching off, or ranting) brings all the issues into the open where they can finally be addressed.

I have one final point to make about opening your mind. You need to stay in the *present* or the now. It is pointless to bring up problems from the *past* or worry about the *future* (which is unknowable).

Don't worry if opening sounds hard; the initial opening—of both heart and mind—can be small but it is a necessary precursor to the next stage.

Holding: When you are both being assertive, both of your needs, wants, and beliefs are equally important. With contemplative thinking, both of your viewpoints are equally valid. For this stage, you need to live without a resolution. I know this is hard because we hate uncertainty (plus comparative thinking—which is all about certainty —is deeply ingrained).

Paul's teenage daughter discovered that her mother was having an affair with a man in the village and told her father. Being a problem-solver by nature, he came up with three solutions for his wife, Lucy. First, she would give up the other man and they would work on their marriage and fall back in love with each other. Second, she could leave and be free to see the other man. Third, if she truly didn't love Paul, they could stay together for the kids and co-parent (but she could not communicate with the other man). When he saw me five days after the discovery, he had given his wife the weekend to make her mind up. I could understand why Paul craved certainty—because he was in agony and wanted it over as soon as possible. So I tried to get Paul to step back for a moment:

"All of the options are fraught with pain and worry because Lucy might lie—it wouldn't be the first time—or she could be filled with good intentions but find it impossible to give up the other man or be seduced into exchanging texts and meeting up again," I explained.

"But surely, one of the options is better than the others," said Paul (which is comparative thinking).

"What if forcing a decision now, and feeling a temporary sense of relief, makes things worse in the medium-term?" I asked him.

"There's a saying in my line of business: it's better to make a wrong decision now than a good one in a month's time. I've always thought that it's a bit crazy," he acknowledged.

Paul decided to take away the ticking clock of a deadline to decide and gave Lucy time and space to present her thoughts on the way forward.

Holding is coping with contradictions, looking at multiple options, living with uncertainty, and approaching the dilemma in a contemplative way. For example: Paul and his daughter needed to know what was going to happen next AND Lucy needed time to decide what she truly wanted. You can tell if a thought is truly contemplative when both positions are treated as equally valid.

Going through: You will probably only understand this stage when you've reached this place yourself. All the previously intractable problems seem to dissolve and you can go through into a solution. There are no winners or losers because everybody is happy. It sounds almost magical and I suppose in some ways it is. So what's going on? First of all, with contemplative thinking, there is enough space for each of you to express yourself and discover your true feelings. Material that was previously unconscious or unsayable comes into the light where it can be properly examined. Often these apparently immovable issues turn out to be built on fear or on out-of-date scripts from your parents—that's why they dissolve relatively easily. Sometimes when you are not challenged, you don't need to hold on so tightly to being right (for fear of being wrong) and an alternative solution emerges into which you can both *go through*. I doubt the decision will be exactly what either of you wanted at the start of the process, but it can be warmly embraced by both of you.

Rex, fifty-four, and his wife Joan, fifty-three, thought they had an intractable problem: How to balance being a couple with being true to themselves. Rex believed that if you loved someone you should want to spend the majority of your time together. Joan agreed but only up to a point: she wanted space to see her friends (sometimes without Rex) and follow separate interests. Their clash revolved around his outdoor interests (sailing and hiking) and her more indoor activities (theater and philosophy). At one point, the tension became too much and they split up for six months. Rex decided to find someone with similar tastes and searched online for a woman who loved sailing as much as he did.

"Except it's a bit like dating myself, we understand each other and we enjoy the same things but there's no spark or connection," he explained.

Joan had been dating too although kept men at arm's length. During the time apart, they had remained in each other's lives as friends: he helped with her tax return and she collected him from hospital after a minor operation. In other words, they were open to each other and instead of trying to solve their differences were able to "hold" them. They had several philosophical discussions about what had been wrong with their marriage:

"I had been expecting Joan to rescue me and fill the void of not feeling loved enough as a child," said Rex.

"My confidence was at an all-time low after the end of my first marriage to my previous husband, and I was looking to Rex to pick me up and sort me out and then got resentful when he did," explained Joan.

"But we've decided instead of expecting each other to 'fix' us, we could sort ourselves out."

These insights were really valuable and would not have been possible without being open to each other, holding the paradoxes for a while and contemplative thinking (which is centred on reserving judgment).

At this point, Rex and Joan were able to "go through" to the other side of their central dilemma.

"We don't have to be together all the time," said Rex.

"I can come sailing when the weather is fine and Rex doesn't have to join my philosophy class."

"We don't even have to live in the same house if we don't want to," added Rex

That's the great advantage of being forty- or fifty-something or beyond, you can do what works for you—not what everybody else thinks you "should" do.

The final resistance I get to contemplative thinking: doesn't there come a point when you have to face that something actually IS wrong? I'm afraid this question underlines our addiction to *comparative* thinking. What I hope is that during the "holding" phase, you will have begun to see the "right" in your partner's "wrong" stance and the differences will begin to dissolve—because your partner will have started to see the "right" in what he or she previously considered your "wrong" position. Ultimately, what matters is not whether something measures up to some opinion of "right" or "wrong"—defined by whom? All sensible people, a survey of all your friends, the Pope, the Dalai Lama?—but whether something works for the two of you.

So how do my partner and I move forward?

If you have been incorporating these skills I've been outlining, you will probably have begun to operate in the opening and holding phases. For example, you will be trying to relate to each other as adult to adult (from Transactional Analysis theory) rather than as critical parent to adapted child. By beginning to take your partner's opinions seriously, you are more likely to listen and ask open questions (How will that work? What will that look like? Why do you feel like that?). If you don't immediately shoot your partner's ideas down, it will encourage him or her to open further. By showing a real interest in what your partner has to say, you are modeling the behavior that you'd like back, which will encourage your partner to reciprocate (rather than starting a race to the bottom, where his or her aggressive behavior prompts the same from you until you reach a bitter divorce.)

If you give yourself enough time in the holding phase, and burrow deeper into the issues between you, you will find that you are starting to *go through*. Don't worry, you will recognize it when it happens.

What if your partner simply refuses to engage? As I'm sure you know, you can't force someone to open (and trying to gets the opposite reaction). So if this is your situation, you probably need to consider the next option:

WOULD A TEMPORARY SEPARATION HELP?

Staying with contemplative thought ... I am not a great fan of temporary separations AND I am not a great fan of not listening to your partner, if he or she is asking for one. And again ... temporary separations can make it harder to communicate because you're not under the same roof AND they can take the pressure off day-to-day living. If your partner is convinced that another man or woman is the answer, a contemplative response would be: it could provide the space to cement their relationship with each other AND it could help them realize that their relationship with the affair partner is built on fantasy.

Set it up properly

Instead of letting everything coming to a head—with your partner walking away out of frustration or you throwing him or her out—focus on talking through how a trial separation could work. Instead of looking for ways to persuade your partner he or she is wrong to need space, ask questions about how a separation might work. What about our finances? What will we tell the children? How often will we see each other? What would make this a constructive time for both of us?

Key idea for saving your relationship: Focus on improving your communication and listening skills because they become even more important when you're not under the same roof.

Have a good idea of how you got into this mess

When you're in a hole, it's a good idea to stop digging. So if your relationship isn't working (at least for one of you), you've got to ask him or her why and really listen to the reasons. Think about your part in the crisis, because even if your partner has been unfaithful—for which you're not to blame—he or she will not have turned from a loving partner to this detached cold figure overnight. Why has he or she put so much distance between you that someone else has been able to come between you?

Key idea for saving your relationship: Every time you meet up with or text your partner think: how could I do this differently? If you just fall into the same old traps or behave in the same old way, you'll get the same old response—and you know where that's got you. I suggest doing the opposite, so if you tend to clam up, speak up. If you usually pour your heart out, try biting your tongue.

Truly give your partner space

Lots of trial separations don't work because the partner who needs space feels that he or she doesn't get it. That's because they are fielding ten texts and five long emails a day or, when their partner comes to collect the children, he or she ends up hanging around the house. I know it's tough because you fear "out of sight is out of mind" (and if that's the case how can you work on your marriage). However, you are at risk of making your partner think true space could only be achieved by ending the relationship.

Key idea for saving your relationship: During the trial separation please put your main focus and energy on working on *yourself*. By this I mean seeking to understand why this is so painful—perhaps to do with your childhood—and learning alternative ways to cope with adversity (rather than sending off a desperate text). If you chase your partner, he or she may flee. If you step back, you could encourage him or her to come forward. This is also a good time to focus on *good*

239

self-care. By this I mean setting aside time for activities you enjoy, seeing friends, and generally unwinding.

Don't read the runes

What makes trial separations so difficult is uncertainty. To protect yourself you will try and second-guess your partner, anticipating how every move will be received (and end up overthinking), and finally let your imagination run riot. This sucks all the joy out of the few face-to-face encounters that you do have because you're interpreting every gesture for clues about the future.

Key idea for saving your relationship: Live for this moment, right now—rather than worrying about the past or trying to guess the future. Can you cope today? Probably, yes. It's when you imagine further ahead than the weekend that you start to panic. So every time you feel yourself unraveling focus back on NOW. Enjoy the view from your window, the cup of coffee you're drinking, or that moment of peace before the kids get back from school (this is mindfulness in action). You will be amazed at how much calmer you'll feel.

Expect setbacks

I reckon I've seen over two thousand clients and I've never met anyone who doesn't have setbacks. It's especially common when the partner who wanted space starts to think about returning that the other, who has been holding out for the relationship, starts to get cold feet. This is a good sign because it means he or she is ready to negotiate for what he or she needs—rather than accepting anything to get his or her partner back—but for the couple it can be really unsettling.

Key idea for saving your relationship: Setbacks are not a problem if you can learn something from them. So what is this bump in the road telling you? What do you need to do differently? If you've reached a dead end, how can you go back and find another way round?

Wait for your partner to talk about the future

If you keep contacting your partner to ask, "How do you feel?" and "How is the trial separation going?", it's not only exasperating but you're reminding your partner that he or she doesn't love you or needs space. I know it's hard but please wait for your partner to talk about the future. Your job is to make today's interactions better.

Key idea for saving your relationship: This is a really tough time and you're going to need help (rather than expecting your partner to make you feel better). So please look for support from friends, family, self-help books, and consider consulting a professional. You're facing one of the biggest challenges of your life but you don't have to do it alone.

EXERCISE   WATCHING YOUR INNER VOICE

In the Tao, one of the world's oldest spiritual philosophies, the three central virtues are *compassion, moderation,* and *humility.* I have been stressing moderation (finding a middle way) and humility (not thinking you have all the answers) but it is equally important to be compassionate—and not just to your partner. *I'd like you to be compassionate to yourself too.*

If your partner has been or is being unfaithful, you've had to deal with a series of terrible shocks. If your partner is depressed, you will have felt alone and unsupported. You will probably have been criticized and condemned by your partner and, after a while, there is a danger that you will begin to believe the criticism.

I hope that reading this book will have provided hope and some ideas for positive changes. However, it's equally possible that by describing the behaviors that exacerbate the middle passage, I could have prompted a further round of self-criticism. (My apologies if this has been the case.)

The real damage is caused by your own inner voice, or self-talk. While it is possible to dismiss your partner's criticism and/or parts of this book (because I don't have all the answers or know what's right for you), it is much harder to ignore the voice in your own head.

- Over the next few days, I'd like you to watch the tone of your self-talk.

- Do you beat yourself up or get angry with yourself when things don't go the way you planned?

- How often can you be compassionate with yourself? By which I mean, calm, kind, and understanding.

- If you find that your self-talk is more negative than compassionate, please don't be self-critical (because adding another negative is not going to make you feel better!).

- Instead, I would just like you to observe the tone of your self-talk rather than judge it. In this way, you can begin to distance yourself from the running commentary in your head and that's the first step away from swallowing it wholesale.

- If you still find it hard, let me offer a couple of maxims: "I'm going through a huge challenge and I'm doing my best" and "It's OK to make mistakes as I can learn from them."

- After a while, you will register when it is negative self-talk, and if you practice being compassionate to yourself, you can gently lead yourself away from this trap and find a more moderate voice.

CONCLUSION

When you've been dealing with an erratic, depressed, or angry partner—and constantly under attack—it is easy to see yourself as a hero or heroine, keeping the show on the road for the sake of the children. I hope my book has shown how that automatically labels your partner as the villain and widens the gap between the two of you. If you can accept that even your partner's wildest claims have *some* legitimacy, albeit greatly exaggerated, you will have made a huge step forward. When you accept the bits that *do* seem reasonable, your partner will stop defending him or herself and the two of you can find different ways of communicating. As you can imagine, this whole process is going to take time. How much? I'm afraid it is impossible to estimate but it will probably be longer than you want or imagine.

Along the way, there will be good days and bad days. During the good, you will probably not even be thinking about the future—just enjoying the moment. During the bad, I suggest putting this period of pain and upset into the context of the whole of your relationship. When you compare two or three tough years against fifteen, twenty, or more happy years together, it doesn't seem quite so bad. I would also focus on getting through today and enjoying the pleasures around you—like the children, a good cup of coffee, or a walk in the park—rather than worrying about tomorrow.

When your partner is closed off, take the opportunity to work on yourself—by which I mean plenty of self-care, building your self-confidence, and not putting off projects that make your life more meaningful. If you are learning about yourself and life in general—plus adding new skills to your repertoire—everything will feel more bearable and more hopeful.

SUMMING UP

➤ With assertiveness both you and your partner's needs are equally important. With contemplative thinking both your viewpoints are equally valid.

➤ If you can "hold" the contradictions and conflicts in both your positions—without trying to convince each other you're right—your differences will begin to melt as you talk more and more. At this point you will "go through" your problems and find a mutually acceptable way forward.

➤ In the meantime, coping with a partner going through the middle passage is a long and tough journey and it's important to be compassionate toward yourself.

PART THREE

Breaking the deadlock

CHAPTER NINE

Coming together

The term midlife crisis suggests a momentary madness before normal service is resumed. In reality, something much deeper is happening. You are facing a relationship crisis (where you discover if your marriage can provide the protection and nurturing that you expected), a career crisis (where you wonder if your work or role provides the fulfillment and satisfaction that you believed it promised), and a crisis of meaning (where you question whether our society's goal of material affluence is working for you, or you wonder whether you are on the right path at all). With overlapping crises, there are often two reactions: Paralysis (where you don't know where to start and risk sinking into depression) or becoming hyper (where any change is better than none and the risk of collateral damage is huge). The best reaction is to look at what was ignored while you were building a clear provisional adult identity for the first half of your life, because these discarded parts can be your friend and teacher in the second:

Doers become Thinkers
Feelers become Doers
Thinkers become Feelers
Extroverts become Introverts
Visionaries become Practical
Practical people long for Vision

247

When I work with my clients through the middle passage—the journey between the first and second half of life—I am asked the same question over and over again: "Does it have to be so painful?" It's an excellent point. All the wisdom we need is freely available; I still have the copy of *The Road Less Traveled* by M. Scott Peck (Simon & Schuster, 1978) that I bought in a bookshop at Dallas airport while killing time between flights. I highlighted the opening lines: "Life is difficult. This is a great truth, one of the greatest truths. It is a great truth because once we truly see this truth, we transcend it." However, they didn't make sense for another fifteen years or so until my partner was dying. I had intellectually known that life was difficult but I had somehow thought that I was immune: I alone, and the people I loved were not going to die (unless they were really, really old). I was a good person and therefore nothing *too* bad was going to happen to me. So back in my twenties, when I read the opening lines, my brain registered them as important and my hand used the highlighter but I didn't really take them in.

Suffering dragged me deeper into myself, opened up another level to my heart, and smashed through a floor to reveal a cavity below. Bereavement forced me to visit the ancient places where old pains had been hidden and to face the emptiness of the comforting rationalizations and the pat narratives I'd been telling myself. Trust me, I didn't want truth. I was perfectly happy with my ordered life, thank you. However as Richard Rohr writes in *Adam's Return: The five promises of male initiation* (Crossroad, 2004), "There is no renewal in all of nature without a proceeding loss."

While being naive in my twenties was probably understandable, if I still believed that life should be easy at fifty-seven I would be profoundly disappointed. So the truth—to quote the closing credits from *The X-Files*—might have been "out there," but you were unlikely to be ready to hear it until faced with a life-changing experience, reaching your forties or fifties, or your partner's crisis turned your life upside down.

THE IMPORTANCE OF COMPASSION

If your partner is going through a midlife crisis, I would like you be compassionate—even though he or she is behaving strangely and hurting you and your children. It is really difficult to answer the three key existential questions: Who am I? What gives my life meaning? What are my values? It is particularly difficult in the modern individualistic world. All the old moral and social certainties about how to behave have been stripped away. This is a great opportunity—because we can do what our soul needs—but it is not surprising that your partner found it hard to come up with his or her own world view from scratch (or that he or she messed everything up along the way). I bet your partner is probably no keener to have reached this point than I was. However something—like my bereavement—has exploded him or her out of the old certainties: perhaps a job loss, an injury, death of a parent, or a financial crises.

You can be compassionate about the original problem, I'm sure, but can you extend that compassion to the inevitable fallout? If the answer is no, perhaps it's time to call a divorce lawyer (because your partner's behavior has become too destructive) or to consider mediation. If the answer is maybe, it sounds like you need a bit more time: to understand your partner better, to digest this book, and do some more talking together. If the answer if yes, please proceed to the final two sections.

If you're going through the middle passage yourself and questioning everything along the way, I would like you to be compassionate toward your partner. Your world is bewildering enough, but just imagine what your partner is going through. If you can't, let me help. It's basically the same as for you but with less control and more stumbling about in the dark.

Obviously I don't know how dismissive your partner is being about your search for a more meaningful life. It could be largely a reaction to your recent actions or because, in your partner's mind, you've brought a third party into play (and violated his or her trust). Can you be compassionate, even in the face of your partner's anger?

If the answer is maybe, it could be that you need more time to digest the book.

If the answer is yes, please keep reading.

THREE KEY SKILLS

If I had to boil down my advice for resolving the conflict between you and your partner, it comes down to integrating the following three skills into how you communicate.

1. **Move into adult-to-adult mode**—rather than being a critical or nurturing parent and a sulky, closed off, rebellious adapted child. Adult-to-adult is about problem solving, staying in the present (rather than dragging up old grievances), or worrying about the future (and the precedent that might be set now). It involves asking lots of open questions which start with why, what, when, who, and how. (If you would like a recap of this idea, see chapters five and six.)

2. **Assertiveness.** Instead of downgrading your needs to please your partner or finding reasons why you are right (and therefore why your needs should be met), an assertive approach values your needs equally. I sum it up in the maxim: *I can ask, you can say no, and we can negotiate.* My advice is to start with smaller day-to-day issues before moving on to the larger more life-changing ones. (If you would like a recap of this idea, see chapter eight.)

3. **Contemplative thinking.** This skill helps you move away from the need to be right (which makes your partner wrong) and keeps your ears and heart open long enough to understand your partner's position and discover that his or her and your opinions are equally valid. Instead of looking for the perfect answer, contemplative thinking draws out the pros and cons, refines the question and goes beyond the polarized all-or-nothing stand-off of comparative thinking. (If you would like a recap of this idea, see chapter six. For an explanation about how to "hold"| the differences and "go through" them, see chapter eight.)

EXERCISE   HOW TO BE MORE CONTEMPLATIVE

Once you become aware of the difference between comparative and contemplative thinking, you will discover how deeply entrenched is the notion of comparing and contrasting in Western thinking and how difficult it is to stop. So here are four ideas to help break the habit:

- *Watch yourself from a distance.* To stop yourself becoming too identified with your private viewing gallery on the world, I recommend keeping a diary. (I did it myself for the year I spent asking: Who am I?). The alternative is to imagine stepping away from yourself and observe yourself from another place in the room.

- *Meditation.* This practice is good for keeping calm but also for training your mind to observe rather than getting caught up in your thoughts.

- *Argue the opposite of a cherished opinion.* We spend a lot of time coming up with evidence of why we're right and our partner is wrong. Worse still, with every restating of our position, we become more fixed in our rightness. So try this philosophy undergraduates' exercise and find the arguments to undermine your position. For example, I'd always thought it was important to follow your dreams but American singer and poet Patti Smith put a convincing case for the opposing idea in a radio interview: "My late husband and I had many dreams. Eighty percent of them we never realized but Fred always said, 'Not all dreams are meant to be realized.' The act of dreaming is its own reward."

- *Adopt a contemplative maxim.* I like this one from Richard Rohr's *Naked Now: Learning to see how the mystics see:* "Wisdom is never just mine but always a shared experience" (Crossroad Publishing Company, 2009). Alternatively, you could make up your own to reflect how everything is a mixture of good and bad, helpful,and unhelpful, endearing, and maddening.

SHOULD I GIVE THIS BOOK TO MY PARTNER?

By now, I hope that you have a glimmer of how life could be. But how do you recruit your partner? Before you decide to share the book, it is best to adopt a few of the ideas first. My suggestion would be to start with the fulsome apology—see chapter six. It should improve the general atmosphere between you and your partner and create a sense of hope. At this point, you're ready to introduce the book by explaining what you've learned about yourself and the elements of partner's behavior that you understand better (and can be more compassionate about).

Please be wary of using me to prove that you are right (and hard done by) and your partner is wrong (and cruel) because it will put more bricks in the wall between you. I would also avoid making threats or conditions—for example, read this book or we're over—because that will close your partner's mind. If your partner is too angry, too besotted with someone else, or too depressed, try to keep talking and communicating better until you reach a good enough place to suggest reading this book.

CONCLUSION

The middle passage is part of the journey from provisional to full adult and becoming your true self rather than what your parents or society expected. In this way, you reap the benefits of the U-shaped life and get the upswing of happiness and fulfillment. The alternative is to distract yourself, self-medicate, and blame (your parents, your partner, your boss, or life in general) and become closed off and cynical. I call this the L-shaped life—as it doesn't bring the benefits of a meaningful old age. But it is easy to get seduced by the false promises of a short-lived boost—a shortcut—and find yourself in the W-shaped life (from where you will still need to climb out of the pit of despair).

Along the journey, it is easy to cause suffering to the people who love you, but the benefit of being forty- or fifty-something is that you are ready to give up the old thinking from the first half of your life—where there are winners or losers—and find a solution that will be accepted by everyone. I hope that will be finding a better and more connected relationship with your partner that works for who you are today. If that is not possible, I hope that you will keep talking—improving your communication—until your separation is a more mutual decision. In this way, you will lay the foundations for being great co-parents rather than spending any more years fighting. If you keep on learning and growing, no experience—however painful—is wasted.

SUMMING UP

➤ Sometimes you have to come close to a breakdown to have a breakthrough.

➤ Compassion will help lower the temperature of a dispute and facilitate more constructive negotiations.

➤ Don't blame each other. No one can keep you from reaching a more meaningful and expansive second half of life but yourself.

Further reading

Wake Up and Change Your Life
(Marshall Method Publishing, 2015)

Whether you've decided your life is no longer working and you need to change or you feel that change has been thrust upon you, I have nine ideas that build into a proven plan for personal transformation. There's an explanation of why change is so tough and how to discover what's really holding you back. Most important, for when you're in crisis, there's advice on how to keep calm. The book also features:

- More on assertiveness and Transactional Analysis (adult-to-adult communication).

- How to move from the drama triangle of the affair into the winner's triangle and build cooperation.

- The importance of boundaries for you and your relationships.

- Understanding the difference between your zone of concern and your zone of control.

- An in-depth explanation about mindfulness and living in the present.

Learn to Love Yourself Enough
(Marshall Method Publishing, 2014)

Both sides of the midlife crisis are tough and can knock your self-esteem, so it's important to look after yourself:

- Don't let other people put you down: recognize the five phases of projection and how understanding our own projections leads to better and happy relationships.

- Reprogram your inner voice: identify the three kinds of negative thinking that work together to undermine self-confidence and whether they are based on fact or just opinion.

- Set realistic goals: learn how perfectionism undermines self-esteem.

- Rebalance yourself: understand that problems lurk in the extremes and why the middle way is the most successful way.

- Conquer fears and setbacks: overcome the day-to-day problems that life and other people throw at you.

- Examine your relationship with your parents: discover the six types of child-parent relationships, and how to accept the legacy of your past.

- Find forgiveness: debunk the two myths about forgiveness and discover what can be gained from negative experiences.

How Can I Ever Trust You Again? (Marshall Method Publishing, 2016)

If your partner has had an affair, my bestselling book covers the seven stages of recovery. It will help make sense of your feelings and reassure you that they are normal and understandable. There's also my detailed plan on how to come out of this crisis with a stronger and better marriage. Each chapter ends with a short section written for the partner who has been unfaithful and many couples find that these sections prompt constructive conversations on how to move forward. The book also includes:

- The eight types of affairs and how understanding your partner's is key to rescuing your relationship.
- How to stop your imagination running wild and your brain going into meltdown.
- How the person who had the affair can help their partner recover.
- What derails recovery and how to get your marriage on track again.

I Can't Get Over My Partner's Affair
(Marshall Method Publishing, 2015)

Recovering from your partner's infidelity or coping with the fear that it's still going on is a really lonely place. Friends and family want to be supportive but they don't truly understand, become so overwhelmed by your upset that they want a quick fix, or they simply lose patience. That's why I've written this compassionate book featuring fifty stories from people on a similar journey and my advice on how to turn each one round. It features:

- How to diagnose why you're feeling stuck.
- The common myths about infidelity that make recovery harder.
- What to do if your partner is still in love with the other man or woman.
- Strategies to stop arguments from going round in circles.
- How to turn the pain of infidelity into something positive.

My Husband Doesn't Love Me and He's Texting Someone Else (Marshall Method Publishing, 2015)

Men fall out of love for different reasons to women and this book will explain the three things every woman needs to know to protect her relationship. It is also full of practical techniques for coming back from the brink—like assertiveness—and advice on diagnosing whether your husband is depressed (plus what to do if he is). In the second half of the book, I tackle what to do if you suspect or know your husband is having an affair:

- The six types of other woman, from "a spark" to "the love of his life."
- Tailored strategies for dealing with each type.
- Five worst and best reactions after uncovering what's really going on.
- How to keep calm even when provoked.
- How to combat the poison that she's slipping into your relationship.
- When to keep fighting and when to make a tactical withdrawal.

My Wife Doesn't Love Me Any More
(Marshall Method Publishing, 2014)

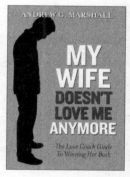

If your life is in turmoil because your wife has just told you that she doesn't love you and your marriage is over, this book will bring a bit of sanity into your world. In my experience, more relationships end at this point not because women are determined to leave but because men panic and end up pushing their wife even further away. In this book, I explain how to keep calm and listen, really listen, rather than arguing or trying to find a magic fix. I also cover:

- How to figure out why she's fallen out of love.
- Five things you think will save your relationship but should absolutely avoid.
- What her words and actions really mean and how to use them to win her back.
- What to do to instantly improve the atmosphere at home.
- How to prevent past mistakes from undermining your attempts to build a better future.
- Five pick-me-up tips for when you're down and need to keep focused.
- When it's time to admit it's over and what factors indicate you should still fight on.

What Is Love? (Marshall Method Publishing, 2014)

Love is one of the most powerful forces in our lives but also one of the most misunderstood. This book combines some of the great minds who have written about love from across the ages plus fifty letters from people just like you. Many of my clients read this book with their partner because it prompts useful discussions about love and relationships without getting caught in the same old loops. Sections include:

- The spark went out.

- Being torn between a partner and a lover.

- Restoring love after an affair.

- Making amends.

I Love You But I'm Not in Love With You (Health Communications Inc., 2007)

Over 100,000 copies sold worldwide. This book will help you get to the roots of why seemingly loving partners detach and how the simple everyday things you thought were protecting your relationship were really undermining it. There is more information about limerence and how to speak your partner's love language. Also includes:

- How to argue productively and address the core of the issue.

- Employ the trigger words for more effective communication.

- Find a balance between being fulfilled as an individual and being one half of a couple.

- Create new bonds instead of searching for old ones.

Have the Sex You Want
(Marshall Method Publishing, 2014)

If your sex life is more about going through the motions than building a connection, this book is for you. It will help you challenge the myths about sex that are stopping passionate lovemaking, break down the bad habits that have accumulated over your years together, and rebuild your sex life into something sensual and more plentiful. At the core is a ten-week proven plan for restoring intimacy which builds slowly until you have the sex you've always wanted. I also show how to:

- Talk about sex with your partner without getting defensive.
- Deal with different levels of desire.
- Understand the three types of making love and how they can rekindle desire.
- Repair the damage from an affair by reconnecting again in the bedroom.

I Love You But You Always Put Me Last
(Health Communications Inc., 2014)

Having children is life-changing and many mothers are often perceived as "controlling" by their partners simply because women are usually the primary caregiver and therefore tend to set the agenda for parenting. At midlife it is helpful to step back and review decisions made when you and the children were younger and whether they are still valid today. I cover:

- Overcoming differences in parenting style and finding acceptable compromises.
- Sharing household responsibilities effectively.
- Providing good relationship role models for your children.
- How to be good partners as well a good parents.

BY OTHER AUTHORS

Middle Passage: From misery to meaning in midlife by James Hollis (Inner City Books, 1993). This book is full of wisdom and insight into being forty- or fifty-something but it assumes a basic knowledge of Jung and his teachings.

Finding Meaning in the Second Half of Life: How to finally, really *grow up* by James Hollis (Avery, 2006). All the Hollis wisdom but aimed at a more general audience.

Iron John: A book about men by Robert Bly (Addison-Wesley, 1990). It is impossible to read this book without getting a strong reaction—sometimes positive and sometimes negative (and often on the same page). If you keep an open mind, and almost read Bly like poetry, you'll probably find some parts speak to you and provide useful insights.

The Drama of Being a Child: The search for the true self by Alice Miller (Virago, 1987). If you're looking for an insight into what happened in your childhood and its long-term impact, this is a great starting point.

What About Me? The struggle for identity in a market-based society by Paul Verhaeghe (Scribe, 2014). This book will put your personal search for meaning into a wider contemporary context.

The Mindful Way Through Depression: Freeing yourself from chronic unhappiness by Mark Williams, John Teasdale, Zindel Segal and Jon Kabat-Zinn (Guilford Press, 2007). A practical self-help book for dealing with depression that comes with some useful guided meditations.

Mindfulness: A practical guide to finding peace in a frantic world by Mark Williams and Danny Penman (Piatkus, 2011). The bestselling introduction to being truly present, coming off autopilot and living in the present—rather than the past or the future.

Tao Te Ching by Lao Tzu with commentary by Rory B Mackay (Blue Star Books, 2014). If you're wondering not just about the meaning of your life but tackling broader spiritual questions this is a good starting point. When quoting from the *Tao Te Ching,* I have used this translation.

The Road to Character by David Brooks (Random House, 2015). A mixture of biography of famous or remarkable people from Saint Augustine to twentieth-century figures (mostly American), and a discussion about why our society is so dissatisfied and lost.

Falling Upward: A spirituality for the two halves of life by Richard Rohr (Joessey-Bass, 2011). Although Rohr writes from a Christian perspective, he is respectful of other faiths and even no faith.

Adam's Return: The five promises of male initiation by Richard Rohr (Crossroad, 2004). This book looks at the joys and the sorrows of being a man and the tough issues of life—like death, suffering, and loss. Although Rohr writes from a position of profound personal belief, he has useful insights even if you have none or are unsure.

TITLES BY ANDREW G. MARSHALL

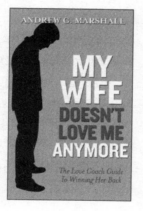

About the author

Andrew G. Marshall is a marital therapist with thirty years of experience. He trained with Relate (the UK's leading couple-counseling charity) but now leads a team in private practice in London and Sussex offering the Marshall Method. He is also the author of seventeen other books on relationships and contributes to the *Mail on Sunday, Sunday Telegraph, Times,* and women's magazines around the world. To date, his work has been translated into over twenty different languages. To receive regular updates about Andrew's books, articles and events, subscribe to his newsletter at www.andrewgmarshall.com.